MW01108446

# How To Heal The Sick

## By
## Smith Wigglesworth

Dr Michael H Yeager

Copyright © 2019 Dr. Michael H Yeager

All rights reserved.

**ISBN:** 9781796506419
**Imprint:** Independently published

## DEDICATION

This is written for those who truly hunger and thirst after all that God has made available through the life, ministry, sufferings, death and resurrection of Jesus Christ . My prayer is that not only will your life be touched by these **divine miraculous occurrences**, but you yourself will truly step in to that realm where all things are possible .God is not a respecter of people, what he did for Smith Wigglesworth, he desires to do for you and me. May you experience wonderful transformation and divine healing.

*These true stories have been modernized in order to make them more understandable and descriptive in our modern vernacular. All of the stories have been compiled from many different articles, books, stories, sermons, and writings of Smith Wigglesworth. There are acknowledgments at the beginning of each chapter to give credit to those who recorded the stories, and wrote them down for the increase and benefit of our personal faith. Jesus Christ is the same yesterday today and forever. What he did for these people he will do for you and me!*

# CONTENTS

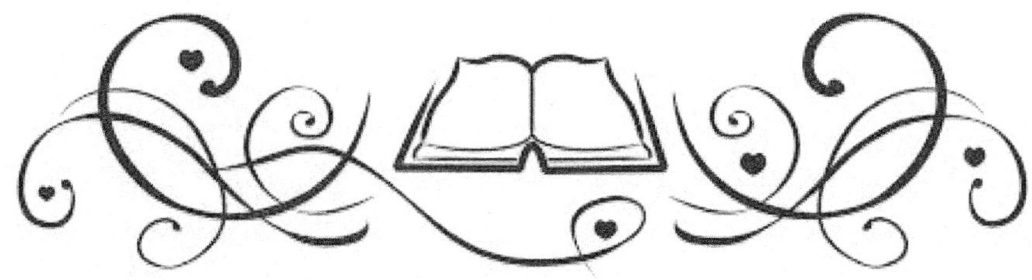

# EXHORTATION

**Smith Wigglesworth: This Is The Place Where God Will Show up!**

**You must come to a place of ashes, a place of helplessness, a place of wholehearted surrender where you do not refer to yourself. You have no justification of your own in regard to anything. You are prepared to be slandered, to be despised by everybody. But because of His personality in you, He reserves you for Himself because you are godly, and He sets you on high because you have known His name (Ps. 91:14). He causes you to be the fruit of His loins and to bring forth His glory so that you will no longer rest in yourself. Your confidence will be in God. Ah, it is lovely. "The Lord is the Spirit; and where the Spirit of the Lord is, there is liberty" (2 Cor. 3:17).**

**Born June 10th, 1859**<br>
**Died March 4th, 1947**

# CHAPTER ONE

## (24) QUOTES ON: DIVINE HEALING

**"When things are not going right, there are satanic forces in operation. What is my solution? To rebuke the condition of sin, death, disease, or whatever it is. I can pray in the Holy Ghost, and that prayer is effectual to bring down every stronghold of the enemy."**

"Because you are joint-heirs, you have a RIGHT to healing for your body & to be delivered from ALL the power of the enemy"

**"The man who is going through with God to be used in healing must be a man of longsuffering."**

"When you were saved, you were saved the moment you believed, and you will be healed the moment you believe."

**"Faith is just the open door through which the Lord comes. Do not say 'I was saved by faith' or 'I was healed by faith'. Faith does not save and heal. God saves and heals through that open door."**

"The Lord does not heal you to go to a baseball game or to a racetrack. He heals you for His glory so that from that moment your life will glorify Him."

God's Word never fails. He will always heal you if you dare to believe Him. Men are searching everywhere today for that with which they can heal themselves, but they ignore the fact that the Balm of Gilead (Jeremiah 8:22) is within easy reach.

**Wigglesworth's reply to a woman who asked for books on healing. 'I handed her my Bible & said: "Matthew, Mark, Luke & John' are the best"**

A woman once asked Wigglesworth to recommend books on healing. 'I handed her my Bible and said "Matthew, Mark, Luke & John are the best"

**Is salvation and healing for all? It is for all who will press in and get their portion. The word can drive every disease away from your body. It is your portion in Christ, Him who is our bread, our life, our health, our all in all."**

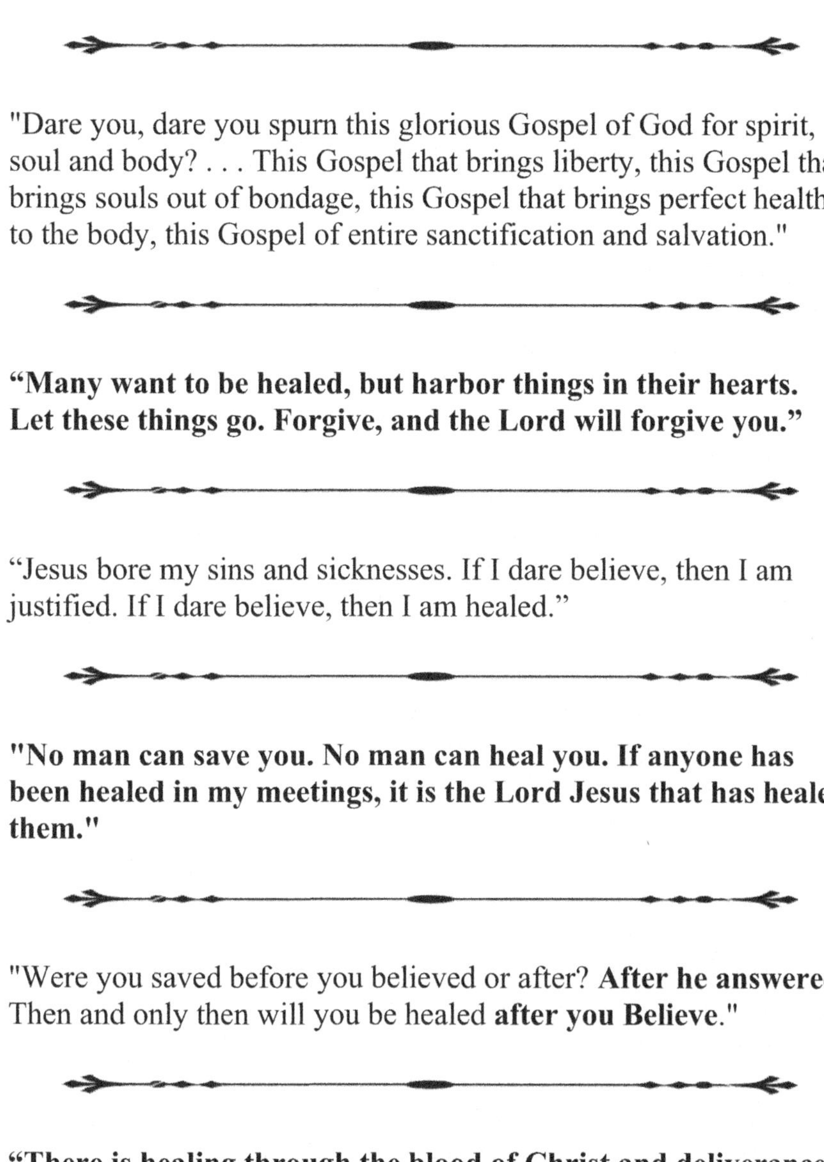

"Dare you, dare you spurn this glorious Gospel of God for spirit, soul and body? . . . This Gospel that brings liberty, this Gospel that brings souls out of bondage, this Gospel that brings perfect health to the body, this Gospel of entire sanctification and salvation."

**"Many want to be healed, but harbor things in their hearts. Let these things go. Forgive, and the Lord will forgive you."**

"Jesus bore my sins and sicknesses. If I dare believe, then I am justified. If I dare believe, then I am healed."

**"No man can save you. No man can heal you. If anyone has been healed in my meetings, it is the Lord Jesus that has healed them."**

"Were you saved before you believed or after? **After he answered**. Then and only then will you be healed **after you Believe**."

**"There is healing through the blood of Christ and deliverance for every captive."**

"You must never treat a cancer case as anything else but a living evil spirit, and this form of disease is one that you must cast out."

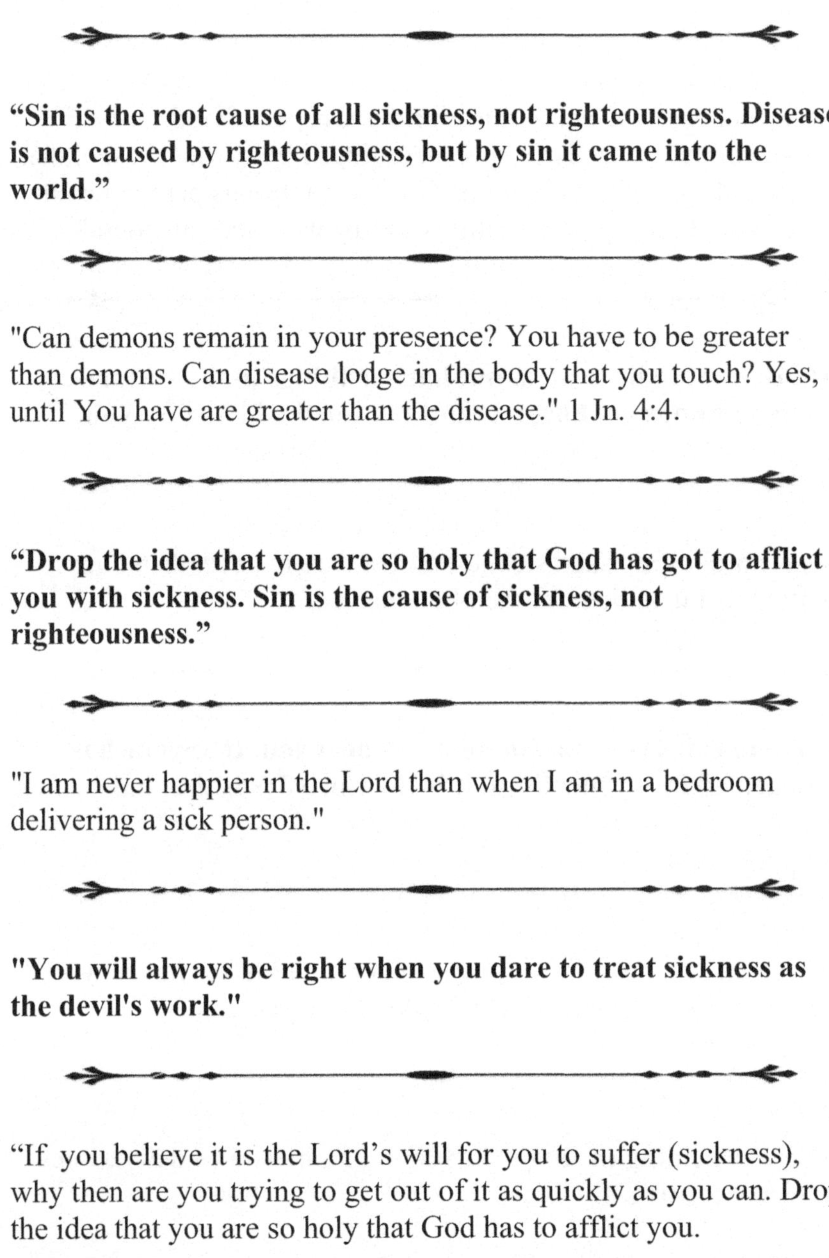

**“Sin is the root cause of all sickness, not righteousness. Disease is not caused by righteousness, but by sin it came into the world.”**

"Can demons remain in your presence? You have to be greater than demons. Can disease lodge in the body that you touch? Yes, until You have are greater than the disease." 1 Jn. 4:4.

**“Drop the idea that you are so holy that God has got to afflict you with sickness. Sin is the cause of sickness, not righteousness.”**

"I am never happier in the Lord than when I am in a bedroom delivering a sick person."

**"You will always be right when you dare to treat sickness as the devil's work."**

“If you believe it is the Lord’s will for you to suffer (sickness), why then are you trying to get out of it as quickly as you can. Drop the idea that you are so holy that God has to afflict you.

**Wigglesworth once told a woman he had a cure for sickness in his bag. When asked to show it, he says ‘I opened my bag &**

**took out my Bible.**

There are those who think I am rather unmerciful in my dealing with the sick. No, I simply have no mercy for the devil.

***WHY PEOPLE ARE SICK**

Where people are in sickness you find frequently that they are dense about Scripture. They usually know three scriptures though. They know about Paul's thorn in the flesh, and that Paul told Timothy to take a little wine for his stomach's sake, and that Paul left someone sick somewhere; they forget his name, and don't remember the name of the place, and don't know where the chapter is. Most people think they have a thorn in the flesh. The chief thing in dealing with a person who is sick is to locate their exact position. As you are ministering under the Spirit's power the Lord will let you see just that which will be more helpful and most faith-inspiring to them.

***WHY MANY BELIEVERS ARE NOT HEALED!**

I realize that God can never bless us on the lines of being hardhearted, critical or unforgiving. This will hinder faith quicker than anything. I remember being at a meeting where there were some people tarrying for the Baptism-seeking for cleansing, for the moment a person is cleansed the Spirit will fall. There was one man with eyes red from weeping bitterly. He said to me, "I shall have to leave. It is no good my staying without I change things. I have written a letter to my brother-in-law, and filled it with hard words, and this thing must first be straightened out." He went home and told his wife, "I'm going to write a letter to your brother and ask him to forgive me for writing to him the way I did." "You fool!" she said. "Never mind," he replied, "this is between God and me, and it has got to be cleared away." He wrote the letter and came again, and straightway God filled him with the Spirit.

I believe there are a great many people who would be healed, but they are harboring things in their hearts that are as a blight. Let these things go. Forgive, and the Lord will forgive you. There are many good people, people that mean well, but they have no power to do anything for God. There is just some little thing that came in their hearts years ago, and their faith has been paralyzed ever since. Bring everything to the light. God will sweep it all away if you will let Him. Let the precious blood of Christ cleanse from all sin. If you will but believe, God will meet you and bring into your lives the sunshine of His love.

**Romans 15:19**
**Through mighty signs and wonders, by the power of the Spirit of God; so that from Jerusalem, and round about unto Illyricum, I have fully preached the gospel of Christ.**

**Galatians 3:5 He therefore that ministereth to you the Spirit, and worketh miracles among you, doeth he it by the works of the law, or by the hearing of faith?**

**Acts 4:33 And with great power gave the apostles witness of the resurrection of the Lord Jesus: and great grace was upon them all.**

**Acts 6:8 And Stephen, full of faith and power, did great wonders and miracles among the people.**

**1 Corinthians 2:4 And my speech and my preaching was not with enticing words of man's wisdom, but in demonstration of the Spirit and of power:[5] That your faith should not stand in the wisdom of men, but in the power of God.**

**From the book: Smith Wigglesworth a man who walked with God by George Stormont**

**#1** I had great compassion for the sick and needy before God ever started using me. One day a group of spiritual leaders came and said to me: "Smith We want to go to the Keswick convention, we have been thinking whom we should leave to do the work. We can only think of you." I said, "I couldn't conduct a healing service." They said, "We have no one else. We trust you to take care of the work while we are away."

A thought came into my mind: "Well, any number of people can talk. All I have to do is to take charge." The following week when I got there the place was full of people. Of course, the first thing I did was to look for someone who would do the speaking; but everyone I asked said, "No, you have been chosen and you must do it." And so I had to begin. I do not remember what I said that night but I do know that when I had finished speaking fifteen people came forward for healing. One of these was a man from Scotland who was hobbled on a pair of crutches. I prayed for him and he was instantly healed. There was no one more surprised than

I was. He was jumping all over the place without his crutches. This encouraged the others who were there to believe God for their healing and all of these people were healed. I am sure it was not my faith, but it was God in His compassion coming to help me in that hour of need.

**#2** The Lord opened the door of faith for me more and more. I announced that I would have a Divine Healing meeting in Bradford on a certain evening. I can remember that there were twelve people who came that night and all of those twelve were miraculously healed. One had a tongue badly bitten in the center through a fall. This one was perfectly healed. Another was a woman with an ulcer on her ankle joint and a large sore that was constantly discharging. She was healed and there was only a scar the next day. The others were healed the same way.

**#4** One day a man asked me, "Does Divine Healing embrace seasickness? "I answered, "Yes. It is a spirit of fear that causes your seasickness, and I command that spirit to go out of you in Jesus' name." He was never seasick again from that day forward, though he had to travel much.

#5 One day a man came to our house. He was a very devoted brother. I said to him, "Mr. Clark, you seem downcast today. What's up?" He answered, "I left my wife dying. Two doctors have been with her right through the night and they say she cannot live long." I said to him, "Why don't you believe God for your wife?" He answered, "Brother Wigglesworth, I cannot believe for her."

He went out of the house broken-hearted. Immediately I went to see a brother named Howe who was opening a small mission in Bradford. I thought he was the right man to go with me, in order to assist me. When I said, “Will you go with me?” he answered, “No, indeed I won’t. Please do not ask me again. But I believe if you will go, God will heal.” I realized then that the Lord put those words in his mouth to encourage me.

Well, I knew a man another brother named Nichols who, if he got the opportunity to pray, would pray all around the world three times and then come back. So I went to him and said, “Will you come with me to pray for Sister Clark?”

He answered, “Yes, I will be very glad.” We had a mile and a half to walk to that house. I told him when he began to pray not to stop until he was finished. When we got to the house we saw that Mrs. Clark was almost dead. I said to the one I had brought with me, “You see the dangerous condition of Sister Clark. Now don’t waste time but begin to pray.” Seeing he had an opportunity, he began.

I had never heard or suffered so much unbelief or unnecessary prayer as I did when he was praying, and I cried to the Lord, “Stop him! Please, Lord, stop this man’s praying.” Why? Because he prayed for the dear husband who was going to be bereaved and for the children who were going to be motherless. He piled it on so thick that I had to cry out, “Stop him, Lord; I cannot stand this.” And thank God, he stopped.

Though I knew that neither Clark nor Nichols believed in Divine Healing, I had concealed a small bottle in my hip pocket that would hold about half a pint of oil. I put a long cork in it so that I could open the bottle easily. I took the bottle out of my pocket and held it behind me, and said: “Now you pray, Mr. Clark.” Brother Clark, being encouraged by Brother Nichols’ prayer, prayed also that he might be sustained in his great bereavement. I could not stand it at all, and I cried, “Lord, stop him.” I was so earnest and so broken that they could hear me outside the house. Thank God, he stopped.

As soon as he stopped, I pulled the cork out of the bottle, and went over to the dying woman who was laid out on the bed. I was very young in the faith when it came to Divine healing at this time and did not know any better, so I poured all of the contents of that bottle of oil over Mrs. Clark's body in the name of Jesus!

I was standing beside her at the top of the bed and looking towards the foot, when suddenly the Lord Jesus Himself appeared to me. I had my eyes open looking right at Him. There He was at the foot of the bed. He gave me one of those gentle smiles. I see Him just now as I tell this story to you. I have never lost that vision, the vision of that beautiful soft smile upon the face of Jesus. After a few moments He vanished but something happened that day that changed my whole life forever. Mrs. Clark was raised up and filled with life. She lived to bring up a number of children; she even outlived her husband by many years.

**1#6** My wife and I were both very zealous for the Lord and spent a great deal of time in open-air meetings. One Sunday a violent pain gripped me so deep it brought me down to the ground. Two men supported me and brought me home. The same thing had happened before but the pain had not been near as severe in previous times. My wife and I prayed all night.

The next morning I said to my wife, "It seems to me that this is my home-call. We have been praying all night, and nothing has happened; I am worse. It does not seem as though anything can be done. You know our agreement is that when we know we have received a home-call, (dyeing) only then to save each other the embarrassment of having an inquest and the condemnation of outsiders, would we call a Doctor. I said to her: to protect yourself you should now call a physician. But I leave it with you to do what you think should be done."

My poor wife was in a sad plight, with all the little children around her and there seemed to be no hope whatever. She began to weep and left me to go and get a physician—not for him to help me, because she did not think he could help me in the least, but believing that the end of my life had come.

When the doctor came he examined me, shook his head, and said, "There is no hope whatever. He has had appendicitis for the past six months and the organs are in such shape that he is beyond hope." He turned to my wife and said, "I have to make a number of calls, Mrs. Wigglesworth. I will come and see you again later. The only hope is for him to have an immediate operation, but I am afraid your husband is too weak for that."

When he left the room, an elderly lady and a young man came to our house. She was a great woman of pray, and she believed that everything that was not of good health was of the Devil.

While she prayed, the young man laid his hands on me and cried out, **"Come out, Devil, in the name of Jesus."**

To my utter surprise I felt at that moment as well as I had ever felt in my life. I was absolutely free from pain. As soon as they had prayed for me they went downstairs, and I got up, believing that no one had a right to remain in bed when healed.

When I got downstairs, my wife cried, "Oh!" I said, "I am healed." She said, "I hope it is true." I inquired, "Any work to be done?" "Yes, there is a woman who is in a great hurry to get some plumbing done; if we could not take care of it, she would have to go somewhere else." She gave me the address and I went out to do this work.

While I was at work, the doctor returned. He put his silk hat on the table, went upstairs, and got as far as the landing, when my wife shouted, "Doctor! Doctor! Doctor!" He asked, "Are you calling me?" "Oh, Doctor, he's not here. He has gone out to work." The doctor answered, "They will bring him back a corpse, as sure as you live.

" Well, the "corpse" has been coming and going around the world preaching the Gospel these many years since that time! I have, laid hands on people with appendicitis in almost every part of the world and never knew of a case not instantly healed, even when doctors were on the premises.

**# 8** In Oakland, Calif., we were having a meeting in a very large theatre. So many came to that place that in order to accommodate everyone we had to have overflow meetings. There was a rising tide of people getting saved in the meeting by rising voluntarily up and down in the place, and getting saved. And then we had a large group of people who needed help in their bodies, rising in faith and being healed.

One of these people was an old man 95 years of age. He had been suffering for three years, till he got to the place where for three weeks he had been taking liquids. He was in a terrible state. I got him to stand while I prayed for him; and he came back, and with a shining face, told us that new life had come into his body.

Later when he testified he had this testimony: He said, "I am 95 years old. When I came into the meeting, I was full of pain from cancer of the stomach. But now I have been so healed that I have been eating perfectly, and have no pain." Many of the people were healed in a similar way.

**#9** In one particular meeting a lady arose who had a bad case of rheumatism in the left leg. After being prayed for, she ran the full length of the hall several times, then testified to partial healing. A young man with pain in the head was healed instantly. Another man with pain in the shoulder was healed instantly also.

**#10** I will never forget the face of a man that came to me one time. His clothes hung from him, his whole frame was shrivelled, and his eyes were glaring and glassy, his jawbones stuck out, his whole being was a manifestation of death. He said to me, "Can you help me?" Could I help him?

I told him if we believe the **Word of God** can we help anybody, but we must be sure we are basing our faith on the Word of God. If we are on the Word of God then what God has promised will happen. I looked at him and I told him that I had never seen anybody that was still alive that looked like him. I said, "What is wrong with you? He answered with a small whisper of a voice, "I had a cancer in my chest. I was operated on and in removing this cancer they also removed my swallower; so now I can breathe but I cannot swallow."

He pulled out a tube about nine inches long with a cup at the top and an opening at the bottom to go into a hole. He showed me that he pressed one part of that into his stomach and poured liquid into the top; it was like he was a walking dead man. I said to him:"

… ***whosoever … shall not doubt in his heart, but shall believe that those things which he saith shall come to pass; he shall have saith" (Mark 11:23).***

Based upon this reality I said to him "You shall have a good supper tonight." But, he said "I cannot swallow." I said, "You shall have a good supper tonight." But he repeated "I cannot swallow." ….. I said, "You shall have a good supper; now go and eat."

When he got home he told his wife that the preacher said he could eat a good supper that night. He said, "If you will get something ready I'll see if I can swallow." His wife prepaired a good supper and he took a mouthful. When he had tried to eat before the food would not go down. But the Word of God said "whatsoever," and this mouthful went down, and more and more went down until he was completely filled up! Then what happened? He went to bed with the joy of the knowledge that he could again swallow, and he awoke the next morning with the same joy! He looked for the hole in his stomach, but God had shut that hole in his stomach up.

**#11** I was taken to see a beautiful nine-year-old boy who was lying on a bed. The mother and father were extremely distraught because he had been lying there in bed for months. They had to lift and feed him; he was like a cold statue with flashing eyes. As soon as I entered the place the Lord revealed to me the cause of the trouble with a word of knowledge, so I said to the mother, "The Lord shows me there is something wrong with his stomach." She said, "Oh no, we have had two physicians and they say it is paralysis of the mind." I said, "God reveals to me it is his stomach." "Oh, no, it isn't. These physicians ought to know, they have x-rayed him."

The gentleman who brought me there said to the mother, "You have sent for this man, it is because of you that he has come, now please allow him to help. I prayed over this boy and laid my hands on his stomach. After I prayed He became sick and vomited up a worm thirteen inches long and was perfectly and completely restored.

**Smith - "Never listen to human plans. God can work mightily when you persist in believing Him in spite of discouragement from the human standpoint. ... I am moved by what I believe. I know this: no man looks at the circumstances if he believes."**

**#12** I know of a situation where six people went into the house of a sick man to pray for him. He was an Episcopalian priest, and he laid in his bed utterly helpless, without even strength to help himself. He had read a little tract about Divine healing and had heard about people praying for the sick, and sent for some of my friends, who, he thought, could pray the prayer of faith. He was anointed according to ***James 5:14***, but, he had no immediate manifestation of healing, he wept bitterly. The six people walked out of the room, somewhat discouraged to see the man lying there in an unchanged condition.

When they were outside, one of the six said, "There is one thing we should have done. I wish you would all go back with me and let's try it." They all went back and got together in a group. This brother said, "Let us whisper the name of **Jesus**." At first when they whispered this wonderful worthy name nothing seemed to happen. But as they continued to whisper, **"Jesus! Jesus! Jesus!**

In Faith , sincerity and Love" the power of God began to fall. As they saw that God was beginning to work, their faith and joy increased; and they whispered the name of **Jesus Christ** louder and louder. As they did so the man suddenly arose from his bed and dressed himself. The secret was simply this, those six people had got their eyes off the sick man, and put their eyes upon the **Lord Jesus** Himself, their faith grasped the power and authority that there is in the name that's above every name of **Jesus Christ** of Nazareth.

**From the book: "Ever Increasing Faith" Sermon Titled: Gifts and Healings**

**#13** I was called at 10 o'clock one night to pray for a young lady given up by the doctor. She was dying of consumption. As I looked, I saw that unless God did something it was impossible for her to live. I turned to the mother and said, "Well, mother, you will have to go to bed." She said, "Oh, I have not changed my clothes for three weeks." I said to the daughters, "You will also have to go to bed," but they did not want to go. It was the same with the son.

I put on my overcoat and said, well if you will not cooperate "Good-bye, I'm leaving." They said, "Oh, don't leave us." I said, "I can do nothing here if you do not go to bed." They said, "Oh, if you will stop, we will all go to bed." I knew that God could not move in the least in an atmosphere of just natural sympathy and unbelief.

They all went to bed and I stayed, and that was surely a battle as I knelt by that bed face to face with death and with the devil. But God can change the hardest situation and make you know that He is almighty.

Then the real fight came. It seemed as though the heavens were brass. I prayed from 11 to 3:30 in the morning. As I was praying I saw the light in this young ladies face leave and she died. The devil said, "Now you are done for. You have come from Bradford and this girl has died on your hands." I said, "It can't be. God did not send me here for nothing. Now this is the time to take a hold of violent Faith." I remembered that passage which said, "Men ought always to pray and not to faint." Death had taken place but I knew that my God was all-powerful, and He that had split the Red Sea is just the same today. It was a time when I would not and could not have "No," for an answer, but in the mist of the fight of faith God said "**Yes**."

I looked at the window and at that moment the face of **Jesus** appeared to me. It seemed as though a million rays of light were coming from His face. As He looked at the one who had just passed away, the colour came back to her face. At that moment she rolled over and fell asleep. Oh my then I had a glorious time. In the morning she woke early, put on a dressing gown and walked to the piano. She started to play and to sing a wonderful song. The mother and the sister and the brother had all come down to listen. The Lord had undertaken. A miracle had been wrought.

**#14** I remember being one day in Lancashire, and going round to see some sick people. I was taken into a house where there was a young woman lying on a bed, a very helpless case. The reason had gone, and many things were manifested there which were satanic and I knew it. She was only a young woman, a beautiful child. The husband, quite a young man, came in with the baby, and he leaned over to kiss the wife.

The moment he did, she threw herself over on the other side, just as a lunatic would do. That was very heart-breaking. Then he took the baby and pressed the baby's lips to the mother. Again another wild kind of thing happened. I asked one who was attending her, "Have you sought anybody to help?" "Oh," they said, "We have had many professionals." "But," I said, "have you no spiritual help?" Her husband stormed out, saying, "Help? You think that we believe in God, after we have had seven weeks of no sleep and these maniac conditions."

Then a young woman of about eighteen or so just grinned at me and passed out of the door. That brought me to a place of compassion for the woman. Something had to be done, no matter what it was. Then with all my faith I began to penetrate the heavens, and I was soon out of that house, I will tell you, for I never saw a man get anything from God who prayed on the earth. If you get anything from God, you will have to reach into heaven; for it is all there.

If you are living in the earth realm and expect things from heaven, they will never come. And as I saw, in the presence of God, the limitations of my faith, there came another faith, a faith that could not be denied, a faith that took the promise, a faith that believed God's Word. And from that presence, I came back again to earth, but not the same man. God gave me a faith that could shake hell and anything else.

I said, "**Come out of her, in the name of Jesus**!" And she rolled over and fell asleep and awoke in fourteen hours perfectly sane and perfectly whole.

**#15** When I was going over to New Zealand and Australia, I had many to see me off. There was an Indian doctor who was riding in the same car with me to the docks. He was very quiet and took in all things that were said on the ship. I began to preach, of course, and the Lord began to work among the people. In the second-class part of the ship there was a young man and his wife who were attendants on a lady and gentleman in the first-class. And as these two young people heard me talking to them privately and otherwise, they were very much impressed. Then the lady they were attending got very sick. In her sickness and her loneliness she could find no relief. They called in the doctor, and the doctor gave her no hope.

And then, when in this strange dilemma –( she was a great Christian Scientist, a preacher of it, and had gone up and down preaching it )-- they thought of me. Knowing the conditions, and what she lived for, that it was late in the day, and that in the condition of her mind she could only receive the simplest words, I said to her, "Now you are very sick, and I won't talk to you about anything save this; I will pray for you in the name of Jesus, and the moment I pray you will be healed."

And the moment I prayed she was healed. That was this like precious faith in operation. Then she was disturbed. Now I could have poured in oil very soon. But I poured in all the bitter truth possible, and for three days I had her on nothing cinders and conviction. I showed her true terrible state, and pointed out to her all her folly and the fallacy of her position. I showed her that there was nothing in Christian Science, that it is a pure lie from the beginning, one of the major deceptions of hell. At best a lie, preaching a lie, and producing a lie.

Then she woke up to her true condition. She became extremely penitent and broken-hearted. But the thing that touched her first was that she had to go to preach the simple gospel of Christ where she had preached Christian Science. She asked me if she had to give up certain things. I won't mention the things, they are too vile. I said, "What you have to do is to see Jesus and take Jesus." When she saw the Lord in His purity, the other things had to go. At the presence of the real Jesus all else goes.

This opened the door to the rest of those on the boat. I had a wonderful opportunity to preach to all of the passengers. As I preached, the power of God fell, conviction came and sinners were saved. People began to follow me into my cabin one after another. God was working in a wonderful way.

In the mist of all of this activity a Indian doctor came. He said, "What shall I do? I cannot use medicine anymore." "Why?" "Oh, your preaching has changed me. But I must have a foundation. Will you spend some time with me?" "Of course I will." Then we went alone and God broke the hardened ground of his heart. This Indian doctor decided that he was going right back to his nation with a new purpose. He had left a practice there. He told me of the great influence he had on many people. He was determined to go back to his practice to preach Jesus Christ.

**#16** A woman came to me in Cardiff, Wales, who was filled with an ulceration. She had fallen in the streets twice through this trouble. She came to the meeting and it seemed as if the evil power within her was trying to kill her right there, for she fell, and the power of the devil was extremely brutal. She was helpless, and it seemed as if she had died right there on the spot. I cried,

"O God, help this woman." Then I rebuked the evil power in the name of Jesus, and instantly right then and there the Lord healed her. She rose up and was so filled with excitement and joy that we could not keep her quiet. She felt the power of God in her body and wanted to testify all the time. After three days she went to another place and began to testify about the Lord's power to heal the sick and the demonically oppressed.

She came to me and said, “I want to tell everyone about the Lord's healing power. Have you no tracts on this subject?” I handed her my Bible and said, “Matthew, Mark, Luke, John--they are the best tracts on healing. They are full of incidents about the power of Jesus. They will never fail to accomplish the work of God if people will believe them.”

# CHAPTER TWO

**Smith - "There is nothing impossible with God. All the impossibility is with us when we measure God by the limitations of our unbelief."**

#17 I had been preaching on this line in Toronto, endeavoring to show that the moment a man believes with all of his heart that God puts into him a reality, a substance, a life; yea, God dwells in him, and with the new birth there comes into us a mighty force that is mightier than all the power of the enemy. Well one of the men who was at this meeting ran right out after the service, and when I got home that night this man was there with a big, distinguishing, tall man. This distinguished -looking man said to me, "Three years ago my nerves became shattered. I can't sleep. I have lost my business. I have lost everything. I am not able to sleep at all and my life is one of misery." I said to him, "Go home and sleep in the name of Jesus." He turned around and seemed reluctant to go; but I said to him, "Go!" and shoved him out of the door.

The next morning he called up on the telephone. He said to my host, “Tell Smith Wigglesworth I slept all night. I want to see him at once.” He came and said, “I'm a new man. I feel I have new life. And now can you get me my money back?” I said, “Everything!” He said, “Tell me how.” I said, “Come to the meeting tonight and I'll tell you.”

The power of God was mightily present in that evening meeting, and he was greatly under conviction. He made for the altar, but fell before he got there. The Lord changed him and everything in him and about him. He is now a successful businessman. All his past failures had come through a lack of the knowledge of God. No matter what troubles you, God can shake the devil out of you, and completely transform you. There is none like Him in all of creation.

**#18** One day I was traveling on a railway train where there were two sick people in the car, a mother and her daughter. I said to them, “Look, I've something in this bag that will cure every affliction in the world. It has never been known to fail.” They became very much interested, and I went on telling them more about this remedy that has never failed to remove disease and sickness.

At last they summoned up courage to ask for a dose. So I opened my bag, took out my Bible, and read them that verse, “I am the Lord that healeth thee.” It never fails. He will heal you if you dare believe Him. Men are searching everywhere today for things with which they can heal themselves, and they ignore the fact that the Balm of Gilead is within easy reach. As I talked about this wonderful Physician, the faith of both mother and daughter reached out to Christ, and as I prayed for them Jesus healed them both, right in the train.

**Smith - “You must come to see how wonderful you are in God and how helpless you are in yourself.”**

**#20** In another place a woman came to me and said, “I have not been able to smell for twenty years; can you do anything for me?” I said, “You will be able to smell tonight.” Could I give anybody that which had been lost for twenty years? Not of myself, but I remembered the Rock on which God's church is built, the Rock Christ Jesus, and His promise to give to His own the power to bind and loose.

We can dare to do anything if we know we have the Word of God hidden in our hearts, submitted to in every regards. In the name of the Lord Jesus I loosed this woman. She ran all the way home. The table was full of all kinds of good food, but she would not touch a thing. She said, “I am having a feast of just being able to smell again!” Praise the Lord for the fact that He Himself, Christ Jesus backs up his own Word and proves the truth of it in these days of unbelief and apostasy.

**Smith - “Faith is just the open door through which the Lord comes. Do not say, ‘I was saved by faith’ or ‘I was healed by faith.’ Faith does not save and heal. God saves and heals through that open door. You believe, and the power of Christ comes.”**

**#21** Another person came and said, “What can you do for me? I have had sixteen operations and have had my ear drums taken out.” I said, “God has not forgotten how to make ear drums.” I anointed her and prayed in the name of Jesus Christ, asking the Lord that her ear drums should be replaced. She was so deaf that I do not think she would have heard had a cannon gone off.

She seemed to be as deaf I prayed as she was before. But she saw other people getting healed and rejoicing. Has God forgotten to be gracious? Was His power just the same? She came the next night and said, “I have come tonight to believe God.” Take care you do not come in any other way. I prayed for her again and commanded her ears to be loosed in the name of Jesus. She believed, and the moment she believed she heard, she ran and jumped upon a chair and began to preach right then and there. Later that night I let a pin drop next to her and she heard it fall. God can give new ear drums to your ears. All things are possible with God.

**#22** As I was looking through my letters one day while in the city of Belfast, a man came up to me and said, "Are you visiting the sick?" He pointed me to go to a certain house and told me to go to it and there I would see a very sick woman. I went to the house and I saw a very helpless woman propped up in bed. I knew that humanly speaking she was beyond all help.

She was breathing with short, sharp breaths as if every breath would be her last. I cried to the Lord and said, "Lord, tell me what to do." The Lord said to me, "Read the fifty-third chapter of Isaiah." I opened my Bible and did as I was told. I read down to the fifth verse of this chapter, when all of a sudden the woman shouted, **"I am healed! I am healed!"** I was amazed at this sudden exclamation and asked her to tell me what had happened.

She said, "Two weeks ago I was cleaning house and I strained my heart very badly. Two physicians have been to see me, but they both told me there was no help. But last night the Lord gave me a vision. I saw you come right into my bedroom. I saw you praying. I saw you open your Bible at the fifty-third chapter of Isaiah. When you got down to the fifth verse and read the words, 'With His stripes we are healed,' I saw myself wonderfully healed. That was a vision, now it is a fact."

.

**#27** I was once traveling from Belgium to England. As I landed I received a request to stop at a place between Harwich and

Colchester. The people were delighted that God had sent me, and told me of a special situation that they wanted me to pray for. They said, "We have a brother here who believes in the Lord, and he is paralyzed from his loins downward. He cannot stand on his legs and he has been twenty years in this condition." They took me to this man and as I saw him there in his chair I put the question to him. "What is the greatest desire in your heart?"

He said, "Oh, if I could only receive the Holy Ghost!" I was somewhat surprised at this answer, and I laid my hands on his head and said, "Receive ye the Holy Ghost." Instantly the power of God fell upon him and he began breathing very heavily. He rolled off the chair and there he lay like a bag of potatoes, utterly helpless. I love it when God is at moving. I like to watch God working. There he was with his great, fat body, and his head was swinging just as though it was on a swivel. Then to our joy he began speaking in a heavenly tongue. I had my eyes glued on him and as I saw the condition of his legs I said, "Those legs can never carry that body."

Then I looked up and said, "Lord, tell me what to do. "The Holy Ghost is the executive of Jesus Christ and the Father. If you want to know the mind of God you must have the Holy Ghost to bring God's latest thought to you and to tell you what to do. The Lord said to me, "Command him in My name to walk" But I missed it. I said to the people there, "Let's see if we can lift him up." But we could not lift him, he was like a ton weight.

I cried, "Oh Lord, forgive me." I repented of doing the wrong thing, and then the Lord said to me again, "Command him to walk." I said to him, "Arise in the name of Jesus." His legs were immediately strengthened. Did he walk? YES! He ran all around. A month after this he walked ten miles and back. He has a Pentecostal work now. When the power of the Holy Ghost is present, things will happen.

**Smith - "Great faith is the product of great fights. Great testimonies are the outcome of great tests. Great triumphs can only come out of**

**great trials."**

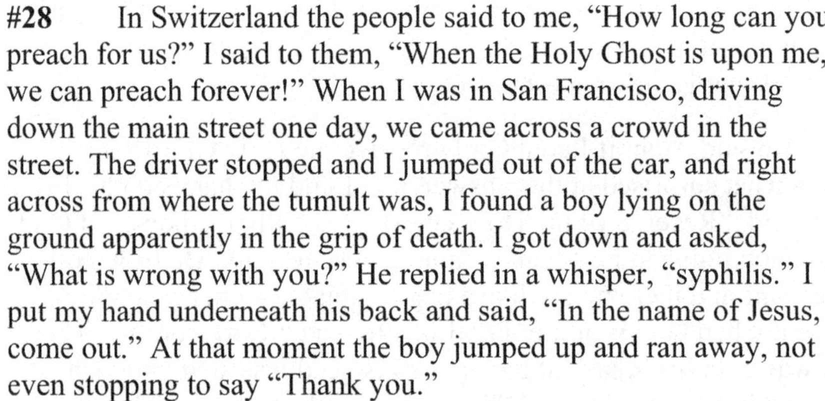

**#28** In Switzerland the people said to me, "How long can you preach for us?" I said to them, "When the Holy Ghost is upon me, we can preach forever!" When I was in San Francisco, driving down the main street one day, we came across a crowd in the street. The driver stopped and I jumped out of the car, and right across from where the tumult was, I found a boy lying on the ground apparently in the grip of death. I got down and asked, "What is wrong with you?" He replied in a whisper, "syphilis." I put my hand underneath his back and said, "In the name of Jesus, come out." At that moment the boy jumped up and ran away, not even stopping to say "Thank you."

**Smith - "Hard things are only opportunities to gain more glory for the Lord as He manifests His power. Every trial is a blessing in disguise.**

**#31** I will tell you what happened in Sydney, Australia. A man with a walking stick passed a friend and me. He had to get down and then twist over, and the tortures on his face made a deep impression on my soul. I asked myself, "Is it right to pass this man?" So I said to my friend, "There is a man in awful distress, and I cannot go any further. I must speak to him." I went over to this man and said to him, "You seem to be in great trouble." "Yes," he said, "I am in terrible shape and will be for the rest of my life."

I said, "You see that hotel. Be in front of that door in five minutes and I will pray for you, and you shall be as straight as any man in in the world." This is a declaration of active faith in Jesus Christ. I came back after paying a bill, and sure enough he was there waiting for me. I will never forget him wondering if he was going to be trapped, or what was up that a man should stop him in the street and tell him he should be made straight. I had said it, so it must be. If you say or declare anything you must stand with God to make it so. Never say anything for bravado, without you having the authority or the right to say it. Always be sure of your foundation, and that you are honoring God.

If there is anything about what you're doing to make you somebody, it will bring you sorrow. Your whole ministry will have to be on the line of humility, grace and blessing. We helped him up the two steps, passed him through to the elevator, and took him upstairs. It seemed difficult to get him from the elevator to my bedroom, as though Satan was making the last effort to take his life, but we got him there. Then in five minutes' time this man walked out of that bedroom as straight as any man has ever walked. He walked perfectly and declared he hadn't a pain in his body.

**#32** In a place in England I was teaching on the lines of faith and what would take place if we believed God. Many wonderful things were happening. When I was done teaching it appeared one man who worked in a coal mine had heard me. He was in trouble with a very stiff knee. He said to his wife, "I cannot help but think every day that that message of Wigglesworth's was to stir us to do something. I cannot get it out of my mind. All the men in the pit know how I walk with a stiff knee, and you know how you have wrapped it around with yards of flannel.

Well, I am going to act. You have to be the congregation." He got his wife in front of him. "I am going to act and do just as Wigglesworth did." He got hold of his leg unmercifully, saying, **"Come out, you devils, come out! In the name of Jesus.** Now, Jesus, help me. **Come out, you devils, come out."** Then he said, "Wife they are gone! Wife, they are gone. This is too good. I am going to act now." So he went to his place of worship and all the other coal workers were there. It was a prayer meeting. As he told them this story these men became delighted. They said, "Jack, come over here and help me." And Jack went. As soon as he was through in one home he was invited to another, delivering and losing these people of the pains they had gotten in the coal mine.

**Smith - "Before God could bring me to this place He has broken me a thousand times. I have wept, I have groaned, I have travailed many a night until God broke me. It seems to me that until God has mowed you down you never can have this longsuffering for others. We can never have the gifts of healing and the working of miracles in operation only as we stand in the divine power that God gives us and we stand believing God, and having done all we still stand believing."**

**#33** I was traveling from Egypt to Italy. God was visiting me wonderfully on this ship, and every hour I was conscious of His blessed presence. A man on the ship suddenly collapsed and his wife was terribly alarmed, and everybody else was panicking. Some said that he was about to expire. But I saw it was just a glorious opportunity for the power of God to be manifested. Oh, what it means to be a flame of fire, to be indwelt by the living Christ!

We are in a bad condition if we have to pray for power when an occasion like this comes along, or if we have to wait until we feel a sense of His presence. The Lord's promise was, "Ye shall receive power after that the Holy Ghost is come upon you," and if we will believe, the power of God will be always manifested when there is a definite need. When you exercise your faith, you will find that there is the greater power in you than that is in the world. Oh, to be awakened out of unbelief into a place of daring for God on the authority of His blessed Book and the redemptive work of Christ!

So right there on board that ship, in the name of Jesus I rebuked the devil, and to the astonishment of the man's wife and the man himself, he was able to stand. He said, "What is this? It is going all over me. I have never felt anything like this before."

From the top of his head to the soles of his feet the power of God shook him. God has given us authority over all the power of the devil. Oh, that we may live in the place where we realize this always, and that were completely submitted to that authority!

**#34** Some years ago I was in Ceylon. In one place the folk complained, "Four days is not enough to be with us." "No," I said, "but it is a better than nothing." They said to me, "We are not touching the multitudes of people who are here." I said, "Can you have a meeting early in the morning, at eight o'clock?" They said they could and would if I so desired. So I said, "Tell all the mothers who want their babies to be healed to come, and all the people over seventy to come, and after that we hope to give an address to the people to make them ready for the Baptism in the Spirit."

It would have done you good to see the four hundred mothers coming at eight o'clock in the morning with their babies, and then to see the hundred and fifty old people, with their white hair, coming to be healed. We need to have something more than smoke and huff and puff to touch the people; we need to be a burning fire for God. His ministers must be flames of fire. In those days there were thousands out to hear the Word of God. I believe there were about three thousand persons crying for mercy at once that day. It was a great sight.

From that first morning on the meetings grew to such an extent that I would estimate every time some 5,000 to 6,000 gathered; and I had to preach in a temperatures of 110 degrees. Then I had to pray for these people who were sick. But I can tell you, a flame of fire can do anything. Things change in the fire.

This was Pentecost. But what moved me more than anything else was this: there were hundreds who tried to touch me, they were so impressed with the power of God that was present. And many testified that with the touch they were healed, It was not that there was any virtue in me—the people's faith was exercised as it was at Jerusalem when they said Peter's shadow would heal them.

**#36** One day as I was waiting for a taxi I stepped into a shoemaker's shop. I had not been there long when I saw a man with a green shade over his eyes, crying pitifully and in great agony. It was heart-rending and the shoemaker told me that the inflammation was burning out his eyes. I jumped up and went to the man and said, "You devil, come out of this man in the name of Jesus."

Instantly the man said, "It is all gone, the pain has left and I can see now." That is the only Scriptural way, to touch the lives of people, and then preach afterwards. You will find as the days go by that the miracles and healings will be manifested. Because the Master was touched with the feeling of the infirmities of the multitudes they instantly gathered around Him to hear what He had to say concerning the Word of God. However, I would rather see one man saved than ten thousand people healed.

**#37** The other day we were going through a very thickly populated part of San Francisco when we noticed a large crowd gathered. I saw it from the window of the car and said I had to get out, which I did. There in the midst was a boy in the agonies of death. As I threw my arms around the boy I asked what the trouble was and he answered that he had terrible cramps.

In the name of Jesus I commanded the devils to come out of him and at once he jumped up and not even taking time to thank me, ran off perfectly healed. We are God's own children, quickened by His Spirit and He has given us power over all the powers of darkness; Christ in us the open evidence of eternal glory, Christ in us the Life, the Truth, and the Way.

**#38** When I was traveling from England to Australia I witnessed for Jesus, and it was not long before I had plenty of room all to myself. If you want a whole seat to yourself just begin to preach Jesus Christ. However, some people listened and began to be truly touched by God. One of the young men said to me, "I have never heard these truths before.

You have so moved me that I must have a longer conversation with you." The young man told me that his wife was a great believer in Christian Science but was very sick now and although she had tried everything she had been unable to get relief, so she was seeing a doctor. But the doctor gave her no hope whatever. When her husband told her about me she became desperate because she was facing the realities of death and she asked that she might have an appointment to meet with me.

When I got to her I felt it would be unwise to say anything about Christian Science so I said, "You are in bad shape." She said, "Yes, the doctors give me no hope." I said, "I will not speak to you about anything but will just lay my hands upon you in the Name of Jesus and when I do you will be healed."

Immediately she was healed and that woke her up and she began to think seriously about her life. For three days she was lamenting over the things she might have to give up. "Will I have to give up the cigarettes?" "No," I said. "Will I have to give up the dance?" and again I replied "No." "Well, we have a little drinking sometimes and then we play cards also. Will I have to give—?" "No," I said, "you will not have to give up anything. Only let us see Jesus."

And right then she got such a vision of her crucified Savior and Jesus was made so real to her that she at once told her friends that she could not play cards any more, could not drink or dance any more, and she said she would have to go back to England to preach against this awful thing, called Christian Science. Oh, what a revelation Jesus gave her!

Now if I had refused to go when called for, saying that I first had to go to my cabin and pray about it, I might have lost this opportunity for a precious woman to be healed and saved. After you have received the Holy Ghost you have power; you don't have to wait.

**Smith - There are 4 principles we need to maintain: 1 READ the Word. 2 CONSUME the Word. 3 BELIEVE the Word. 4 ACT on the Word.**

**#40** A woman in Paris suffered from epileptic fits for over 23 years and could not go out alone. She was instantly delivered healed and can now go out alone. The mother of this girl, too, was healed because of the testimony of her daughter.

**#41** A young man, 27 years of age, was dumb. He came to a meeting sneering and laughing, and came very close to see what was going on. I thought he was seeking God, and put my hands on him. The power of God went through him.

I said to him, "Shout, shout, shout!" and the people called out to him in his language, "Shout!" and for the first time in his life he began to shout. God gave him his speech even though he had been a mocker.

**#42** Police in Switzerland. There were more people night after night seeking healing than there are attending this Convention. We were working until midnight. So many people were healed that two policemen were sent to apprehend me. They said I was doing it without credentials. The police wanted to see a wicked woman who had been healed of a rupture, and was the means of bringing others to be healed. When they heard this they said they wished all preachers did the same.

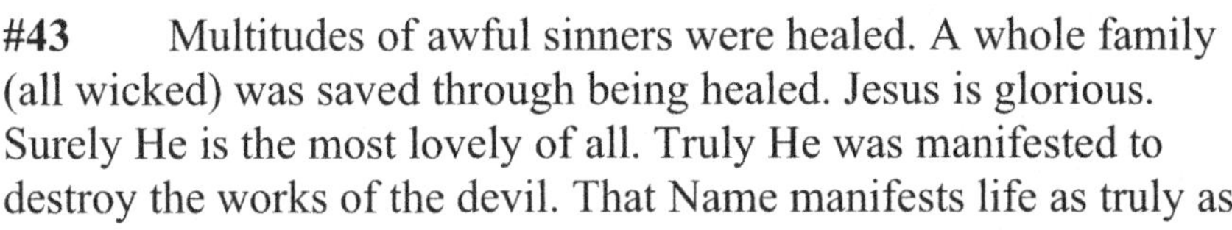

**#43** Multitudes of awful sinners were healed. A whole family (all wicked) was saved through being healed. Jesus is glorious. Surely He is the most lovely of all. Truly He was manifested to destroy the works of the devil. That Name manifests life as truly as ever it did.

**#44** There was a woman with an awful distorted face (nose). I felt an awful sensation, as I do when I see cancer. I rebuked the disease in the Name of Jesus. The next night I forgot about the woman. She came to the meeting and when I saw her I said, "Oh, God! Oh, God!" The same nose shone like glass, and all the skin was new. Our God is a God of love. Who can describe His majesty and glory. Well might the poet say, "Crown Him with many crowns." We must do it. We must do it.

**#45** There was a man with an incurable disease. The moment hands were laid on him he was perfectly healed, after 34 years of suffering from the work of Satan.

**#46** The presence of God was so gloriously manifested. A man on the railway was healed of a disease of 22 years. There was a wicked man healed. He was so broken in spirit that we had to break up the meeting till he got saved. He was going to tell everybody how he was saved. I tell you, there is something in healing. Like the man at the beautiful gate, when the people saw him leaping and praising God 5,000 were saved. God forbid we should glory in anything less than putting Jesus before anyone.

**#47** I was taken to a place to see a girl whose bowels, the doctor said, were completely destroyed. No one could do anything for her. She was in a complete hopeless situation. Immediately she felt an inward power surging through her body as hands were laid upon her. She was gloriously healed by the power and the authority of the name of Jesus.

**#49** A woman came to be healed of a terrible cancer. How it did smell—but God healed her instantly. The husband got saved and the whole family with him. I believe there is a crown for all believers, but it will have to be fought for. There was a young woman vomiting blood. God awakened me in the middle of the night, and in the Name of Jesus I commanded the demon power to come out, and she was immediately healed. It is all in the precious name of Jesus Christ.

**#50** At Zurich it was just the same. God worked amazing special miracles and wonders. The Holy Ghost is different to everyone else. ***"The anointing ye have received abides within you."*** There was a man with a disease you could not look at. I praise God for what Jesus does. In just ten minutes he was made whole. The man sat up in bed and said, "I know I am healed." The doctor came exactly at that time. He was amazed, and said to the man's wife, "Your husband is whole. Whatever has happened? It will not be necessary for me to come anymore." He had been attending his patient three times a day.

**#51** A little boy four years of age was very ill. The doctor who had been attending him for several days said there was something terribly wrong with his brain. The Lord showed me the mischief was in the stomach area, so I laid hands on the child's stomach. A few hours later a worm, fifteen inches long, came out of his mouth, and the boy was made completely whole. Does God know? Hebrews 4:12-13. The discernment of God goes to every part of you—neither is there any creature not manifest in His sight.

**#52** In Ireland a woman had her thigh broken in two places. She lay in bed and could just reach the mantel-piece. When I laid hands on her she said, "It's going right down." "What is going right down?" "The power of God." And in His strength she arose from that bed of affliction completely healed in the name of Jesus.

**#53** I remember one night, being in the north of England and going around to see some sick people, I was taken into a house where there was a young woman lying on her bed, a very helpless case. Her reason was gone and many things were manifested that were absolutely Satanic, and I knew it.

She was a beautiful young woman. Her husband was quite a young man. He came in with a baby in his arms, leaned over and kissed his wife. The moment he did so she threw herself over on the other side of the bed, just as a lunatic would do, with no consciousness of the presence of her husband.

It was heart-breaking, The husband took the baby and pressed the baby's lips to the mother. Again there was a wild frenzy. I said, to the sister who was attending her, "Have you anybody to help?" She answered, "We have done everything we could." I said, "Have you no spiritual help?" Her husband stormed and said, "Spiritual help? Do you think we believe in God after we have had seven weeks of no sleep and this maniac condition? If you think we believe in God, you are mistaken. You have come to the wrong house."

There was a young woman about eighteen who grinned at me as she passed out of the door, as much as to say, "You cannot do anything." But this brought me to a place of compassion for this poor young woman. And then with what faith I had I began to penetrate the heavens. I was soon out on the heights, and I tell you I never saw a man get anything from God who prayed on the earth level. If you get anything from God you will have to pray right into heaven, for all you want is there. If you are living an earthly life, all taken up with sensual things, and expect things from heaven, they will never come. God wants us to be a heavenly people, seated with Him in the heavenlies, and laying hold of all the things in heaven that are at our disposal.

I saw there, in the presence of that demented girl, limitations to my faith; but as I prayed there came another faith into my heart that could not be denied, a faith that grasped the promises, a faith that believed God's Word.

I came from the presence of the glory back to earth. I was not the same man. I confronted the same conditions I had seen before, but in the name of Jesus. With a faith that could shake hell and move anything else, I cried to the demon power that was making this young woman a maniac, "Come out of her, in the name of Jesus!" She rolled over and fell asleep, and awakened in fourteen hours, perfectly sane and perfectly whole.

**#56** A needy man came to me in a meeting. He was withered and wasted, in a hopeless condition; death lay in his eyes. He was so helpless he had to have someone on each side to carry him along. He said to me in a whisper, "Can you help me?"

This afflicted man, standing before me so helpless, so withered, he had had cancer of the stomach. The physicians had taken away the cancer from his stomach, but in removing it they had taken away the man's ability to swallow. The cancer was removed, and seemingly his life was spared, but he could not swallow any longer. In order to keep him from starving, they had made an opening in his stomach and inserted a tube about nine inches long, with a cup at the top, and he fed himself with liquids. For three months he had managed to keep alive, walking about like a skeleton. Here he was asking whether I could help him. What should I say? I remembered the promise, "If thou canst believe, all things are possible to him that believeth." And again, "He that believeth on me, the works that I do shall he do also; and greater works than these shall he do; because I go unto my Father."

The Word must be true. Jesus is with the Father, and therefore even greater works than His can be done if we believe. So I believed, and therefore I spoke.

"Go home and have a good supper," I said. The poor fellow replied, "I cannot swallow." I repeated, "On the authority of the Word of God I say it. It is the promise of Jesus. Go home in the name of Jesus, and have a good supper." He went home. Supper was prepared. Many times before this he had taken food in his mouth and had been forced to spit it out again. But I had believed God. (I am here to inspire you.)

I am a natural man, just as you are, but I dared to believe that he would swallow that night. So after he had filled his mouth with food, he chewed it, and then it went right down his throat. He ate until he was quite satisfied. He and his family went to bed filled with joy. The next morning when they arose they were filled with the same joy. Life had begun again, it seemed. The man looked down to see the opening which the physicians had made into his stomach, but it was gone.

He did not need two openings, so when God opened the natural passage He closed the other. That is what God is like all the time. He brings things to pass when we believe and trust him. God wants you to realize this truth. Dare to believe, then dare to speak, and you shall have whatsoever you say.

# CHAPTER THREE

**#57** A woman came up to me one night and asked, “do you think that I will be able to hear again?” She said, “I have had several operations, and the innards of my ears have been taken away. Is it possible for me ever to hear again?”

I said, “If God has not forgotten how to make the innards for your ears you can hear again.” Do you think God has forgotten? There is one thing God does forget—He forgets our sins when He forgives us—but He has not forgotten how to make the innards for ears. She went away rejoicing and hearing in the name of Jesus.

**Smith - The willingness of God to answer prayer is much greater than the willingness of men to pray!**

**#58** A woman told me that her lungs were completely shredded, and that she could vomit up a pint of pus at any time.

But when I invited people to receive divine healing, she stepped forward and dared to believe God, and she was completely healed in that very meeting by the power of Christ.

**#59** Not long ago I was in a meeting and the power of God was present in a remarkable way. I told the people that they could be healed without coming to the platform. I said that if they would rise and stand upon their feet wherever they were, I would pray and the Lord would heal them. There was a man who put up his hands. I said, "Can't that man rise?" They said he could not, so they lifted him up. We prayed, and that man was instantly healed then and there. His ribs had been broken and were not joined, but God healed him completely.

**#60** When it was evident that this crippled up man was healed, there was such faith throughout the congregation that a little girl said, "Please, gentleman, come to me." I could not see her, she was so small. The mother said, "My little girl wants you to come." So I went over to her. The girl was about fourteen years old, and she was a cripple.

With tears running down her face, she asked, "Will you pray for me?" I said, "Will you dare to believe?" She answered, **"Oh, yes."** I prayed, and placed my hands on her head, in the name of Jesus. The girl said, "Mother, I am being healed. Take these leg braces off—take them all off." The mother loosed the straps and bands on the girl's legs. There was an iron on her foot about 3½ inches deep. She said, "Mother, I am sure I am healed. Take it all off."

So her mother unstrapped the iron and took it off, and that girl began to walk up and down with total freedom. There was not a dry eyes in that place as the people saw that girl walk about with legs quite as true as when she was born. God had healed her right away. What did it? She dared to believe, and trusted God. "Please, gentleman, come to me," she had said. Her longing had been coupled with faith.

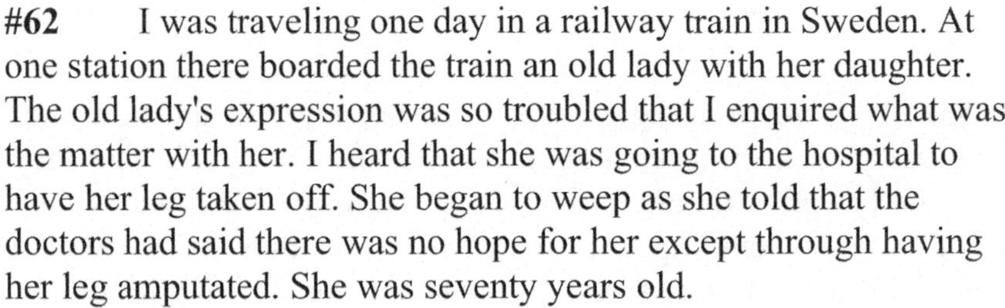

**#62** I was traveling one day in a railway train in Sweden. At one station there boarded the train an old lady with her daughter. The old lady's expression was so troubled that I enquired what was the matter with her. I heard that she was going to the hospital to have her leg taken off. She began to weep as she told that the doctors had said there was no hope for her except through having her leg amputated. She was seventy years old.

I said to my interpreter, "Tell her that Jesus can heal her." The instant this was said to her, it was as though a veil was taken off her face, it became so light. We stopped at another station and the carriage filled up with people. There was a rush of men to board that train and the devil said, "You're done for now. There's no way you can pray with all of these people here" But I knew I had God working with me, for hard things are always opportunities to give the Lord more glory when He manifests His power. Every trial is a blessing.

There have been times when I have been pressed through circumstances and it seemed as if a dozen road engines were going over me, but I have found that the hardest things are just the right opportunities for the grace of God to work. We have such a lovely Jesus. He always proves Himself to be such a mighty Deliverer. He never fails to plan the best things for us.

The train began moving and I crouched down, and in the name of Jesus commanded the disease to leave. The old lady cried, "I'm healed. I know I'm healed." She stamped her leg and said, "I'm going to prove it." So when we stopped at another station she marched up and down, and shouted, "I'm not going to the hospital." Once again our wonderful Jesus had proven Himself a Healer of the broken-hearted, a Deliverer of one that was bound.

**#63** At one time I was so bound that no human power could help me. My wife was looking for me to pass away. There was no help. At that time I had just had a faint glimpse of Jesus as the Healer. For six months I had been suffering from appendicitis, occasionally getting temporary relief. I went to the mission of which I was pastor, but I was brought to the floor in terrible and awful agony, and they brought me home to my bed.

All night I was praying, pleading for deliverance, but none came. My wife was sure it was my home call and sent for a physician. He said that there was no possible chance for me-my body was too weak. Having had the appendicitis for six months, my whole system was drained, and, because of that, he thought that it was too late for an operation. He left my wife in a state of broken-heartedness.

After he left, there came to our door a young man and an old lady. I knew that she was a woman of real prayer. They came upstairs to my room. This young man jumped on the bed and commanded the evil spirit to come out of me. He shouted, ***"Come out, you devil; I command you to come out in the name of Jesus!"*** There was no chance for an argument, or for me to tell him that I would never believe that there was a devil inside of me. The thing had to go in the name of Jesus, and it went, and I was instantly healed.

I arose and dressed and went downstairs. I was still in the plumbing business, and I asked my wife, "Is there any work in? I am all right now, and I am going to work." I found there was a certain job to be done and I picked up my tools and went off to do it. Just after I left, the doctor came in, put his hat down in the hall, and walked up to the bedroom. But the invalid was not there. "Where is Mr. Wigglesworth ?" he asked. "Oh, doctor, he's gone out to work," said my wife. "You'll never see him alive again," said the doctor; "they'll bring him back a corpse."

Well, I'm the corpse. Since that time, in many parts of the world, the Lord has given me the privilege of praying for people with appendicitis; and I have seen a great many people up and dressed within a quarter of an hour from the time I prayed for them. We have a living Christ who is willing to meet people on every line.

**Smith - People search everywhere today for things with which they can heal themselves & ignore the fact that the Balm of Gilead is within easy reach**

**#64** A number of years ago I met Brother D. W. Kerr and he gave me a letter of introduction to a brother in Zion City named Cook. I took his letter to Brother Cook, and he said, "God has sent you here." He gave me the addresses of six people and asked me to go and pray for them and meet him again at 12 o'clock. I got back at about 12:30 and he told me about a young man who was to be married the following Monday.

His sweetheart was in Zion City dying of appendicitis. I went to the house and found that the physician had just been there and had pronounced that there was no hope. The mother was nearly out of her mind and was pulling her hair, and saying, "Is there no deliverance!" I said to her, "Woman, believe God and your daughter will be healed and be up and dressed in fifteen minutes." But the mother just went on screaming.

They took me into the bedroom, and I prayed for the girl and commanded the evil spirit to depart in the name of Jesus. She cried, "I am healed." I said to her, "Do you want me to believe that you are healed? If you are healed, get up." She said, "You get out of the room, and I'll get up." In less than ten minutes the doctor came in. He wanted to know what had happened. She said, "A man came in and prayed for me, and I'm healed."

The doctor pressed his finger right in the place that had been so sore, and the girl neither moaned nor cried. He said, **"This is God."** It made no difference whether he acknowledged it or not, I knew that God had worked. Our God is real in saving and healing power today. Our Jesus is just the same, yesterday, and today, and forever. He saves and heals today just as of old, and He wants to be your Savior and your Healer.

**#65** I was once at an afternoon meeting. The Lord had been graciously with us and many had been healed by the power of God. Most of the people had gone home and I was left alone, when I saw a young man who was evidently hanging back to have a word. I asked, "What do you want?" He said, "I wonder if I could ask you to pray for me." I said, "What's the trouble?" He said, "Can't you smell?"

The young fellow had gone into sin and was suffering the consequences. He said, "I have been turned out of two hospitals. I am broken out all over. I have abscesses all over me." And I could see that he had a bad breaking out at the nose. He said, "I heard you preach, and could not understand about this healing business, and was wondering if there was any hope for me."

I said to him, "Do you know Jesus?" He did not know the first thing about salvation, but I said to him, "Stand still." I placed my hands on his head and then on his clothes which were over the top of his loins and cursed that terrible disease in the name of Jesus.

He cried out, "I know I'm healed. I can feel a warmth and a glow all over me." I said, "Who did it?" He said, "Your prayers." I said, "**No, it was Jesus**!" He said, "Was it He? **Oh, Jesus! Jesus! Jesus**, save me." And that young man went away healed and saved. Oh, what a merciful God we have! What a wonderful Jesus is ours!

**#67** In a meeting a young man stood up, a pitiful object, with a face full of sorrow.

I said, "What is it, young man?" He said he was unable to work, because he could barely walk. He said, "I am so helpless. I have consumption and a weak heart, and my body is full of pain."

I said, "I will pray for you." I said to the people, "As I pray for this young man, I want you to look at his face and see it change."

As I prayed his face changed and there was a wonderful transformation. I said to him, now "Go out and run a mile and come back to the meeting."

He came back and said, "I can now breathe freely."

These meetings continuing but I did not seem any longer. After a few days I saw him again in the meeting. I said, "Young man, tell the people what God has done for you."

"Oh," he said, "I have been back to work. I bought some papers to sell and I have made $4.50." Praise God, this wonderful stream of salvation never runs dry. You can take a deep drink, it is close to you. It is a river that is running deep and there is plenty for all who are thirsty.

**#68** In a meeting a man rose and said, "Will you touch me, I am in a terrible way. I have a family of children, and through an accident in the in the coal mines and I have had no work for two years. I cannot open my hands."

I was full of sorrow for this poor man and something happened which had never come before. We are in the infancy of this wonderful outpouring of the Holy Spirit and there is so much more for us. I put out my hand, and before my hands reached his, he was loosed and made perfectly free.

**Smith - Wigglesworth once told a woman he had a cure for sickness in his bag. When asked to show it, he says 'I opened my bag & took out my Bible.**

**#69** Once a woman stood up in one of our meetings asking for prayer. I prayed for her and she was instantly healed. She cried out, "It is a miracle! It is a miracle! It is a miracle!" That is what God wants to do for every one of us all the time. As soon as we get free in the Holy Ghost something will happen.

**#71** When you deal with a cancer case, recognize that it is a living evil spirit that is trying to destroy the victim's body and snuff out their life. I had to pray for a woman in Los Angeles one time who was suffering with cancer, and as soon as it was cursed it stopped bleeding. It was dead.

The next thing that happened was that the natural body expelled it because the natural body had no room for dead matter. It came out like a great big ball with tens of thousands of fibers. All these fibers had been pressing into the flesh. These evil powers move to get further hold of the system, but the moment they are destroyed their hold is gone. Jesus said to His disciples that He gave them power to loose and power to bind. It is our privilege in the power of the Holy Ghost to lose the prisoners of Satan and to let the oppressed go free.

**#72** I was called to a certain town in Norway. The hall seated approximately 1500 people. When I got to the place it was packed to the roof, and hundreds were trying to get in. There were some policemen there. The first thing I did was to preach to the people outside the building. Then I said to the policemen, "It hurts me very much that there are more people outside than inside and I feel I must preach to the people.

I would like you to get me the market place to preach in." They secured for me a great park and a big stand was erected and I was able to preach to thousands. After the preaching we had some amazing cases of healing. One man came a hundred miles bringing his food with him. He had not been passing anything through his stomach for over a month as he had a great cancer in his stomach. He was healed instantly at that meeting, and opening his parcel, he began eating before all the people.

There was a young woman there with a stiff hand. Instead of the mother making the child use her arm she had allowed the child to keep the arm dormant until it was stiff, and she had grown up to be a young woman and was like the woman that was bowed down with the spirit of infirmity. As she stood before me I cursed the spirit of infirmity in the name of Jesus. It was instantly cast out and the arm was free. Then she waved it all over.

At the close of the meeting the devil laid out two people with epileptic fits, When the devil is manifesting himself, then is the time to deal with him. Both of these people were wonderfully delivered, and they both stood up and thanked and praised the Lord. What a wonderful time we had.

**TEACHING FROM SMITH WIGGLESWOTH**

## * How does Satan get an opening into a believers life?

When the saint ceases to seek after holiness, purity, righteousness, truth; when he ceases to pray, stops reading the Word and gives way to carnal appetites, then it is that Satan comes. So often sickness comes as a result of disobedience. David said, "Before I was afflicted, I went astray."

Seek the Lord and He will sanctify every thought, every act, till your whole being is ablaze with holy purity and your one desire will be for Him who has created you in holiness. Oh, this holiness! Can we be made pure? We can. Every inbred sin must go. God can cleanse away every evil thought. Can we have a hatred for sin and a love for righteousness? Yes, God will create within thee a pure heart. He will take away the stony heart out of the flesh. He will sprinkle thee with clean water and thou shalt be cleansed from all thy filthiness. When will He do it? When you seek Him for such inward purity.

**#73** Everything I have seen in Switzerland has brought me to a place of brokenness before God. At Bern I have stood in a place which has been packed with a multitude of people. I sold moved by God that I ended up weeping as I have seen the needs of the people and then God gave us victory. Hundreds have been saved by the power of God. At Neuchatel God was working marvelously and the devil worked in between, but God is greater than all the Devils and the demons combined together.

At my second visit to Neuchatel the largest theater was hired and it was packed, and God moved upon the people, and on an average 100 souls were saved each night, and many healed through God's touch, yet many did not have the Pentecostal teaching, and one man actually had meetings in opposition at places, but who Is the man who dares to put his hand on the child of God? This man also had prayer meetings to try to prevent people from going to the meetings, but they all turned to nothing but confusion. People came to be ministered to.

**#74** The Holy Ghost is preparing us for some wonderful event. I feel a burning in my bones. I preached one night on Eph. 3 for 3½ hours, and so powerful was the Word that the people did not seem inclined to move. I preached and prayed with the sick until 11:30 p.m. Four people brought a man who was paralyzed and blind; the power of God fell upon him and us and he now walks and sees and is praising God. I have not been to one meeting where the power of God has not been upon us. I say this to His glory.

**#75** At Bern there is a band of praying people. Truly we have seen wonderful things. A girl was brought to me sitting in a chair. I would not minister at first, but told her she must wait and hear the Word of God. Her mother who had come with her was greatly moved as she listened to God's Word being expounded. I then laid hands on the girl, who had never walked. The power of God worked and she now walks. Another case, where a man had had a cancer taken out of his neck, after which he could no longer eat, not being able to swallow. He told me he could not even swallow the juice of a cherry. He had a pipe inserted in his neck so that food could be poured through it into his stomach. I said to him, "You will eat tonight." I prayed with him. He came the next day. I saw that the color had come back into his face, and he told me he had been eating, and could swallow comfortably. He had looked for the hole where the pipe had been inserted in his neck but could not find It. God had completely healed him. He was well known; he was a tea grower and people said he had come to life again. When the Son of God touches a man he does come to life.

**#76** A man came to me suffering from diabetes. The power of God was upon me and I realized that God was working upon this man. I said God has healed you. We took his address and then we checked up on him. He went to the doctor to be examined because he knew he was healed and asked him to examine him. He did so and stated that he was unable to find any trace of the disease whatever. He asked the doctor to give him a certificate which he did and I personally saw it.

**#77** A young woman was dying of consumption, and her doctor had given her up. I laid hands on her in the name of Jesus and immediately she knew that the disease had passed from her body. This girl went to the doctor, who examined her and said,

"Whatever has taken place, you have no consumption now." She replied, "Doctor I have been prayed over; can I tell the people I am healed?" And he said, "Yes, and that I could not heal you." "If I am to tell will you put it in black and white?" And he gave her a certificate which I saw. God had healed her.

**#78** A man was brought into one of the meetings in a wheel chair. He could not walk except by the aid of two sticks, and even then his locomotion was very slow. I saw him in that helpless condition, and told him about Jesus Christ. Oh, that wonderful name! Glory to God! "They shall call His name Jesus." I placed my hands upon his head and said, "In the name of Jesus thou art made whole." This helpless man cried out "It is done, it is done, Glory to God, it is done!" And he walked out of the building perfectly healed. The man who brought him in the wheel chair and the children said that father so and so Is walking. Praise the Lord He is the same yesterday, today and forever.

**#79** I have had some wonderful times in Belfast, Ireland, and in fact all over Ireland. I was in Belfast one day when a young man approached me and said: "Brother Wigglesworth, I am very much distressed," and he told me why. They had an old lady in their assembly who used to pray heaven down upon them. She had an accident. Her thigh was broken and they took her away to the infirmary.

They put her in a plaster of Paris cast and she was in that condition for five months. Then they broke the cast and lifted her on to her feet and asked her to walk. She fell again and broke her leg in another place. To their dismay they discovered that the first break had never knitted together. They brought her home and laid her on the couch and the young man asked me to go and pray for her. When I got into the house I asked: "Do you believe that God can heal you?" She said "Yes. When I heard you had come to the city I thought, 'This is my chance to be healed.'

"An old man, her husband, was sitting in a chair, had been sitting there for four years; helpless. And he said : "I do not believe. I will not believe. She was the only help I had. She has been taken away with a broken leg, and they have brought her back with her leg broken twice. How can I believe God?"

I turned to her and said: "Now is this correct? Yes," she said, "it is the truth." The right leg was broken in two parts. Physicians can join up bones beautifully, and make them fit together, but if God doesn't come in with His healing power, there is no physician who can heal them.

As soon as the oil was placed upon her head and hands laid on, instantly down the right limb there was a stream of life, and she knew it. She said: "I am healed." I said: "If you are healed, you do not need anybody to help you." So I left the room. Immediately after I left she took hold of the mantle shelf above her head and pulled herself up and walked all around the room. She was perfectly healed.

The old man said: "Make me walk." I said: "You old sinner, repent." Then he began: "You know, Lord, I didn't mean it." I really believe he was in earnest, and to show you the mercy and compassion of God, the moment I laid hands upon him, the power of God went thru him and he rose up after four years being in that chair and walked around the room. That day both he and his wife were made whole.

**#80** I was having some meetings in Belfast, and this is the rising tide of what I believe was the move of the Spirit in a certain direction, to show the greatness of that which was to follow. Night after night the Lord had led me on certain lines of truth. There was so much in it that people did not want to go home, and every night until ten o'clock we were opening up the Word of God. They came to me and said: "Brother, we have been feasting and are so full we are we are about ready to burst. Don't you think it is time to call an altar service?"

I said I knew that God was working and the time would come when the altar service would be called, but we would have to get the mind of the Lord upon it. There was nothing more said. They began early in the afternoon to bring the sick people. We never had a thing said about it. The meeting came and every seat was taken up, the window sills were filled and every nook and corner. The glory of God filled the place.

It was the easiest thing in the world to preach; it came forth like a river, and the power of God rested mightily upon everyone. There were a lot of people who had been seeking the baptism of the Holy Ghost for years. Sinners were in the meeting, and sick people. What happened? God hears me say this: There was a certain moment in that meeting when every sick person was healed, every lame person was healed, and every sinner saved, and it all took place in five minutes. There comes into a meeting sometimes something we cannot understand, and it is amazing how God shows up.

**#81** I want all you people to totally delivered, all to be filled with peace, all to be without pain or sickness, I want all to be free. There is a man here with great pain in his head, I am going to lay my hands on him in the name of Jesus and he shall tell you what God has done, I believe that would be the right thing to do, before I begin to preach to you, to help this poor man so that he shall enjoy the meeting like us, without any pain. (The man referred to was in pain with his head wrapped up in a bandage), and after he was prayed for he testified that he had absolutely no pain.

**#82** A man came to me in one of my meetings who had

seen other people healed and wanted to be healed, too. He explained that his arm had been fixed in a certain position for many years and he could not move it. I said to him "Got any faith?". He said He had a lot of faith.

After prayer he was able to swing his arm round and round. But he was not satisfied and complained, "I feel a little bit of trouble just there," pointing to a certain place. "Do you know what is the trouble with you I said to him?" He answered, "No." I said, "Imperfect faith." "What things so ever ye desire, when ye pray, believe that ye receive them and ye shall have them."

**#83** I realize that God can never bless us when we are hardhearted, critical or unforgiving. This will hinder faith quicker than anything in the world. I remember being at a meeting where there were some people waiting for God for the Baptism-seeking for cleansing, for the moment a person is cleansed the Spirit will fall. There was one man with eyes red from weeping bitterly.

He said to me, "I shall have to leave. It is no good my staying without I change things. I have written a letter to my brother-in-law, and filled it with hard words, and this thing must first be taken care of" He went home and told his wife, "I'm going to write a letter to your brother and ask him to forgive me for writing to him the way I did." "You fool!" she said. "Never mind," he replied, "this is between God and me, and it has got to be dealt with." He wrote the letter and came again, and straightway God filled him with the Spirit.

I believe there are a great many people who would be healed, but they are harboring things in their hearts that is grieving the Holy Spirit. Let these things be dealt with in your heart. Forgive, and the Lord will forgive you. There are many good people, people that mean well, but they have no power to do anything for God. There is just some little thing that came in their hearts years ago, and their faith has been paralyzed ever since. Bring everything to the light. God will wash it all away with his blood if you will let Him. Let the precious blood of Christ cleanse you from all sin. If you will but believe, God will meet you and bring into your lives the sunshine of His love.

**Smith - "One half of the trouble in the assemblies is the people's murmuring over the conditions they are in. The Bible teaches us not to murmur. If you reach that standard, you will never murmur anymore. You will be above murmuring. You will be in the place where God is absolutely the exchanger of thought, the exchanger of actions, and the exchanger of your inward purity. He will be purifying you all the time and lifting you higher, and you will know you are not of this world (John 15:19)."**

**#84** Mrs. E. Curtis of Christchurch, New Zealand, was suffering with septic poisoning in the blood. She had become only a skeleton and the doctors could do nothing for her. She had agonizing pains all day and all night. She was healed immediately when prayer was made for her in the name of Jesus. She states that for the past sixteen years she has been afflicted by severe pain but is now wonderfully well.

Another testified to healing of deafness, goiter, adenoids and bad eyesight. Another testified to healing of double curvature of the spine from infancy, hip disease, weak heart, leg lengthened three inches, which grew normal like the other leg. It was also three inches less in circumference. She wore a large boot but now walks on even feet, the large boot having been discarded. Another was healed from a goiter through a handkerchief that had been prayed on. .

# CHAPTER FOUR

**#87** When I was in Australia a man came up to me. He was leaning on a big stick and said, "I would like you to help me. It will take you about an half an hour to pray for me." I said, "Believe God and in one moment you will be whole." His faith was quickened to receive an immediate healing and he went away glorifying God for a miraculous healing. The word of the Lord is sufficient today. If you will dare to believe God's Word you will see a performance of His Word that will be truly wonderful.

**#89** One year ago my husband was instantly healed of double rupture of 3 years' standing, dropsy (2 years), a weak heart, and tobacco chewing (47 years), and praise the Lord, it was all taken away when the power of heaven went straight through him. Nine weeks ago today we went to Portland, Oregon, to hear Brother Smith Wigglesworth, and my husband was healed instantly of heavy blood-pressure and varicose veins which had broken in his ankles and for a year had to be dressed twice a day. No doctor could help him, but, praise God, Jesus was the doctor and healed him. Should anyone wish to write me, I shall be glad to hear from them and will answer all letters.-Mrs. Frank Nephews, 202 E. 1st St., Newberg, Ore.

## Sermon: I Am the Lord That

**#90** One day I had been visiting the sick, and was with a friend of mine, an architect, when I saw a young man from his office coming down the road in a car, and holding in his hand a telegram. It contained a very urgent request that we go immediately to pray for a man who was dying. We went off in an auto as fast as possible and in about an hour and a half reached a large house in the country where the man who was dying resided. There were two staircases in that house, and it was extremely convenient, for the doctors could go up and down one, and my friend and I could go up and down the other, and so we had no occasion to meet.

I found on arrival that had been physically hurt. The man's body had been broken, he was ruptured, and his bowels had been punctured in two places. The discharge from the bowels had formed abscesses, and blood poisoning had set in. The man's face had turned green. Two doctors were in attendance, but they saw that the case was beyond their power. They had telegraphed to London for a great specialist, and, when we arrived, they were at the railway station awaiting for this physician's arrival.

The man was very near death when we arrived and could not speak. I said to his wife, "If you desire, we will anoint and pray for him in the name of Jesus." She said, "That is why I sent for you." I anointed him in the name of the Lord and asked the Lord to raise him up. At that moment there was no change. (God often hides what He does. From day to day we find that God is doing wonderful things, and we receive reports of healings that have taken place that we heard nothing about at the time of our meetings. Only last night a woman came into the meeting suffering terribly. Her whole arm was filled with poison, and her blood was so poisoned that it was certain to bring her to her death. We rebuked the thing, and she was here this morning and told us that she was without pain and had slept all night, a thing she had not done for two months. To God be all the praise. You will find He will do this kind of thing all the time.)

As soon as we anointed and prayed for this brother we went down the back staircase and the three doctors came up the front staircase. As we arrived downstairs, I said to my friend who had come with me, "Friend let me have hold of your hands." We held each other's hands, and I said to him, "Look to God and let us agree together, according to Matthew 18:19, that this man shall be brought out of this death." We took the whole situation before God, and said, "Father, we believe."

Then the conflict began. The wife came down to us and said, "The doctors have got all their instruments out and they are about to operate on him." I cried, "**What**? Look here, he's your husband, and I tell you this, if those men operate on him, he will die. Go back and tell them you cannot allow it." She went back to the doctors and said, "Give me ten minutes." They said, "We can't afford to, the man is dying and it is your husband's only chance." She said, "I want ten minutes, and you don't touch him until I have those 10 minutes."

They went downstairs by one staircase and we went up by the other. I said to the woman, "This man is your husband, and he cannot speak for himself. It is now the time for you to put your whole trust in God and prove Him wholly true. You can save him from a thousand doctors. You must stand with God and for God in this critical hour." After that, we came down and the doctors went up. The wife faced those three doctors and said, "You will not touch my man's body. He is my husband. I am sure that if you operate on him he will die, but he will live if you don't touch him."

Suddenly the man in the bed spoke. "God has done it," he said.

They rolled back the bed clothes and the doctors examined him, and the abscesses were cut clear away. The nurse cleaned the place where they had been. The doctors could see the bowels still open and they said to the wife, "We know that you have great faith, and we can see that a miracle has taken place. But you must let us unite these broken parts and put in silver tubes, and we know that your husband will be all right after that, and it need not interfere with your faith at all." She said to them, "God has done the first thing and He can do the rest. No man shall touch him now." And God healed the whole thing. That same man is well and strong today. I can give his name and address to any who want it.

**#91** My boys did not know anything else but to trust the Lord as the family Physician, and my youngest boy, George, cried out from the attic, "Dadda, come." I cried, "I cannot come. The whole thing is because of me. I shall have to repent and ask the Lord to forgive me." I made up my mind to humble myself before the whole church.

Then I rushed to the attic and laid my hands on my boy in the name of Jesus. I placed my hands on his head and the pain left and went lower down; he cried again, "Put your hands still lower." At last the pain went right down to the feet and as I placed my hand on the feet be was completely delivered. Some evil power had evidently gotten a hold of him and as I laid my hands on the different parts of the body it left. (We have to see the difference between anointing the sick and casting out demons.) God will always be gracious when we humble ourselves before Him and come to a place of brokenness of spirit.

**#92** I was at a place one time ministering to a sick woman, and she said, "I'm very sick. I become all right for an hour, and then I have another attack." I saw that it was an evil power that was attacking her, and I learned something in that hour that I had never learned before. As I moved my hand down her body in the name of the Lord that evil power seemed to move just ahead of my hands and as I moved them down further and further the evil power went right out of her body and never returned.

**#93** I was in Havre in France and the power of God was being mightily manifested. A Greek named Felix attended the meeting and became very zealous for God. He was very anxious to get all the Catholics he could to the meeting in order that they should see that God was graciously visiting France. He found a certain bed-ridden woman who was fixed in a certain position and could not move, and he told her about the Lord healing at the meetings and that he would get me to come if she wished. She said, "My husband is a Catholic and he would never allow anyone who was not a Catholic to see me."

She asked her husband to allow me to come and told him what Felix had told her about the power of God working in our midst. He said, "I will have no Protestant enter my house." She said, "You know the doctors cannot help me, and the priests cannot help, won't you let this man of God pray for me?" He finally consented and I went to the house. The simplicity of this woman and her child-like faith were beautiful to see.

I showed her my oil bottle and said to her, "Here is oil. It is a symbol of the Holy Ghost. When that comes upon you, the Holy Ghost will begin to work, and the Lord will raise you up." And God did something the moment the oil fell upon her. I looked toward the window and I saw Jesus. (I have seen Him often. There is no painting that is anywhere near like Him, no artist can ever depict the beauty of my lovely Lord.) The woman felt the power of God in her body and cried, "I'm free, my hands are free, my shoulders are free, and oh, I see Jesus! I'm free! I'm free!"

The vision vanished and the woman sat up in bed. Her legs were still bound, and I said to her, "I'll put my hands over your legs and you will be free entirely." And as I put my hands on those legs (they were covered with bed clothes), I looked and saw the Lord again. She saw Him too and cried, "He's there again. I'm free! I'm free!" She rose from her bed and walked round the room praising God, and we were all in tears as we saw His wonderful works. The Lord shall raise them up when all the right conditions are met.

**Smith - "I do not ever ask Smith Wigglesworth how he feels!" I simply jump out of bed every morning! I dance before the Lord for at least 10 to 12 minutes – high speed dancing. I jump up and down and run around my room telling God how great he is, how wonderful He is, how glad I am to be associated with Him and to be His child."**

**#96** If I am filled with the Holy Ghost, He will formulate the word that will come into my heart. The sound of my voice is only by the breath that goes through it. When I was in a little room at Bern waiting for my passport, I found a lot of people, but I couldn't speak to them. So I got hold of three men and pulled them unto me. They stared, but I got them on their knees. Then we prayed, and the revival began. I couldn't talk to them, but I could show them the way to talk to Someone else.

God will move upon the people to make them see the glory of God just as it was when Jesus walked in this world, and I believe the Holy Ghost will do special wonders and miracles in these last days. I was taken to see a young woman who was very ill. The young man who showed me the way said, "I am afraid we shall not be able to do much here, because of her mother, and the doctors are coming."

I said, "This is what God has brought me here for," and when I prayed the young woman was instantly healed by the power of God. God the Holy Ghost says in our hearts today that it is only He who can do it. After that we got crowds, and I ministered to the sick among them for two hours.

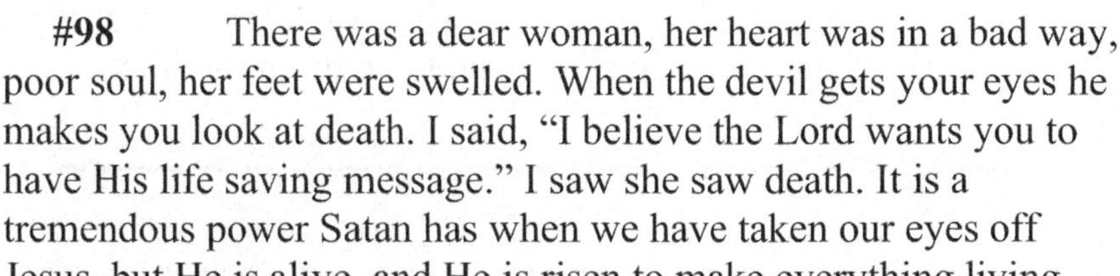

**#98** There was a dear woman, her heart was in a bad way, poor soul, her feet were swelled. When the devil gets your eyes he makes you look at death. I said, "I believe the Lord wants you to have His life saving message." I saw she saw death. It is a tremendous power Satan has when we have taken our eyes off Jesus, but He is alive, and He is risen to make everything living, and His glory is life for evermore.

I thought I would show this dear woman that He has the keys and she might take the promise for a new heart (Psalm 91) and "with long life will I satisfy him." "Oh," she said, "it is a new word to me." "Yes," I said, "all revelation is new." In 3 days God did wonders. She had risen right into the condition of this life. She said, "It is Amen, I have a new heart, my legs are not swelled." It is no good without it is the Amen from above. The Amen—what does it mean—"let it be." It was Jesus who said it—it was He who was Clothed who said it—The One from heaven, the One who had won the victory, and God wants us to do it in His place.

**#99** Last week I went into a house where they were very much in great distress. A young woman was there who, they told me, had not been able to drink for six years. Her body had been rapidly degrading, but the Lord had inspired her with faith and she said to her father, "O Father, I ought to have relief to-day. Somehow I feel this whole trouble ought to go to-day." I knew what it was. It was a demon in the throat.

I believe that the devil is at the bottom of practically every evil in human lives. It was a serious thing to see that beautiful young woman, who, because of this one thing in her life, was so disorganized in her mind and body. I knew it was the power of Satan. How did I know? Because it attacked her at a vital point, and the thing had preyed on her mind and she was filled with fear so that she said, "I dare not drink, for if I do I shall choke."

Deliverance to the captives. I asked the father and mother to go out of the room and then I said to the young woman, "You will be free and drink as much as you want when I have done with you if you will only believe. As sure as you are there you will drink as much as you want." I said further, "Our brethren are going out in the streets to preach to-night and I shall be among them, and in our preaching we will say definitely, 'Every one that will believe on the Lord Jesus Christ can be saved.'

We will also tell them that everyone that believes can be healed. The Word of God shows us plainly that the Son of God bore our sins and our sicknesses at Calvary. They will emphasize it over and over again. It is just as true to say, 'Himself took our infirmities and bare our sicknesses,' as it is to say, 'He was wounded for our transgressions, He was bruised for our iniquities.' " So I said to her, "Now do you believe?" She said, "Yes, I believe that in the name of Jesus you can cast the evil power out." I then laid my hands on her in the name of Jesus. "It is done, you drink."

She went out laughingly and drew the first glass of water and drank. She cried out, "Mother! Father! Brother! I have drunk one glass!" There was joy in the house. What did it? It was the living faith of the Son of God. Oh, if we only knew how rich we are, and how near we are to the Fountain of life. "All things are possible to him that believeth."

**#100** I remember in the year 1920 after a most distressing voyage I went straight from the ship on which I had been traveling to a meeting. As I entered the building a man fell down across the doorway in a seizure. The Spirit of the Lord was upon me and I commanded the demon to leave him immediately. Some years later I visited this same assembly, and I ventured to ask if anyone remembered the incident. A man stood up and I told him to come to the platform. He told me that on that day he had been delivered by the name of Jesus and had not had a seizure since.

**Smith - "Because you are joint-heirs, you have a RIGHT to healing for your body & to be delivered from ALL the power of the enemy"**

**#101** I remember a man coming to me suffering with cancer, who said he had been twelve years in this terrible pain. The power of the Lord was present to heal the sick, and that night he came back to the meeting with all his sores dried up.

**#102** When I was in Orebro 12 years ago I ministered to a girl who was twelve years' old, and blind. When I last went to Orebro they told me that she had had perfect sight from that day forward. The Lord Himself challenges us to believe Him when He says, "Have faith in God." "Verily, I say unto you, That whosoever shall say unto this mountain., Be thou removed, and be thou cast into the sea; and shall not doubt in his heart, but shall believe that those things which he saith shall come to pass; he shall have whatsoever he saith." Did you get that? "He shall have whatsoever he saith." When you speak in faith your desire is an accomplished reality. Our Lord further said, "Therefore I say unto you, What things soever ye desire, when ye pray, believe that ye receive them, and ye shall have them."

**#103** In one place a man said to me, "You helped a good many today, but you have not helped me." I said, "What is the trouble?' He said, "I cannot sleep, and I am losing my mind." I said to him, "Believe." And then I told him to go home and sleep, and I told him I would believe God with him. He went home and his wife said to him, "Well, did you see the preacher?" And he said, "He helped everyone but me." However, he fell asleep when his head hit the pillow. His wife said, "I wonder if it is all right." Morning, noon, and night he was still asleep, but he woke up bright and happy, rested and restored. What had brought about this restoration? Faith in God! "He shall have whatsoever he saith."

**Smith - "No man can save you. No man can heal you. If anyone has been healed in my meetings, it is the Lord that has healed them."**

**#108** While ministering in one place, we had a banquet for people who were diseased--people who were lame and weary, blind and sick in every way. A dear man got hold of a boy who was encased in iron from top to bottom, lifted him up, and placed him onto the platform. Hands were laid on him in the name of Jesus.

"Papa! Papa! Papa!" the boy said. "It's going all over me! Oh, Papa, come and take these irons off!" I do like to hear children speak; they say such wonderful things. The father took the irons off, and the life of God had gone all over the boy!

Don't you know this is the resurrection touch? This is the divine life; this is what God has brought us into. Let it go over us, Lord--the power of the Holy Spirit, the resurrection of heaven, the sweetness of Your blessing, the joy of the Lord!

**#109** One day I was having a meeting in Bury, in Lancashire, England. A young woman was present who came from a place called Rams bottom, to be healed of a goiter. Before she came she said, "I am going to be healed of this goiter, mother." After one meeting she came forward and was prayed for.

The next meeting she got up and testified that she had been wonderfully healed, and she said, "I shall be so happy to go and tell mother that I have been wonderfully healed." She went to her home and testified how wonderfully she had been healed, and the next year when we were having the convention she came again. To the natural view it looked as though the goiter was just as big as ever; but that young woman was believing God and she was soon on her feet giving her testimony, and saying, "I was here last year and the Lord wonderfully healed me.

I want to tell you that this has been the best year of my life." She seemed to be greatly blessed in that meeting and she went home to testify more strongly than ever that the Lord had healed her. She believed God. The third year she was at the meeting again, and some people who looked at her said, "How big that goiter has become." But when the time came for testimony she was up on her feet and testified, "Two years ago the Lord graciously healed me of goiter. Oh I had a most wonderful healing. It is grand to be healed by the power of God."

That day someone remonstrated with her and said, "People will think there is something the matter with you. Why don't you look in the glass? You will see your goiter is bigger than ever." That good woman went to the Lord about it and said, "Lord, you so wonderfully healed me two years ago. Won't you show all the people that you healed me." She went to sleep peacefully that night still believing God and when she came down the next day there was not a trace or a mark of that goiter.

**#110** One day I was preaching and a man brought a boy who was all wrapped up in bandages. The boy was in irons and it was impossible for him to walk and it was difficult for them to get him to the platform. They passed him over about six seats. The power of the Lord was present to heal the sick and it entered right into the child as I placed my hands on him. The child cried, "Daddy, it is going all over me." They stripped the boy and found nothing imperfect in him.

**#113** Not long ago I received a wire asking me if I would go to Liverpool. There was a woman with cancer and gallstones, and she was very much discouraged. If I know God is sending me, my faith rises. The woman said, "I have no hope." I said, "Well, I have not come from Bradford to go home with a bad report."

God said to me, "Establish her in the fact of the new birth." When she had the assurance that her sin was gone and she was born again, she said, "That's everything to me. The cancer is nothing now. I have got Jesus." The battle was won. God delivered her from her sin, from her sickness, and she was free, up and dressed, and happy in Jesus. When God speaks, it is as a nail in a sure place.

Will you believe, and will you receive Him? Life and immortality is ours in the gospel. This is our inheritance through the blood of Jesus—life for evermore!

**YOU DO NOT NEED drugs, quacks, pills and plasters**

We have a big God. We have a wonderful Jesus. We have a glorious Comforter. God's canopy is over you and will cover you at all times, preserving you from evil. Under His wings shalt thou trust. The Word of God is living and powerful and in its treasures you will find eternal life. If you dare trust this wonderful Lord, this Lord of life, you will find in Him everything you need.

So many are tampering with drugs, quacks, pills and plasters. Clear them all out and believe God. It is sufficient to believe God. You will find that if you dare trust Him, He will never fail. "The prayer of faith shall save the sick, and the LORD shall raise him up." Do you trust Him? He is worthy to be trusted.

**#123** One morning about eleven o'clock I saw a woman who was suffering with a tumor. She would be dead before the end of the day. A little blind girl led me to her bedside. Compassion overwhelmed me and I wanted that woman to live for the child's sake. I said to the woman, "Do you want to live?" She could not speak. She just moved her finger. I anointed her with oil and said, "In the name of Jesus." There was a stillness of death that followed; and the pastor, looking at the woman, said to me, "She is gone."

When God pours in His compassion it has resurrection power in it. I carried that woman across the room, put her against a wardrobe, and held her there. I said, "In the name of Jesus, spirit of death, come out." And soon her body began to tremble like a leaf. "In Jesus' name, walk," I said. I stepped away from her body. She did walk and went back to bed.

I told this story in the assembly. There was a doctor there and he said, I am going to investigate this story." He went to the woman this happened to and she told him it was perfectly true. She said, "I was in heaven, and I saw countless numbers all like Jesus. Then I heard a voice saying, 'Walk, in the name of Jesus.'"

There is power in the name of Jesus. Let us apprehend it, the power of His resurrection, the power of His compassion, the power of His love. Love will overcome the most difficult situations - there is nothing it cannot conquer.

**#124** One day I went up into the mountain to pray. I had a wonderful day. It was one of the high mountains of Wales. I heard of one man going up this mountain to pray, and the Spirit of the Lord met him so wonderfully that his face shone like that of an angel when he came back. Everyone in the village was talking about it. As I went up to this mountain and spent the day in the presence of the Lord, His wonderful power seemed to envelop, saturate, overwhelm and fill me.

Two years before this time there had come to our house two lads from Wales. They were just ordinary lads, but they became very zealous for God. They came to our mission and saw some of the works of God. They said to me, "We would not be surprised if the Lord brings you down to Wales to raise up our Lazarus." They explained that the leader of their assembly was a man who had spent his days working in a tin mine and his nights preaching, and the result was that he had collapsed, gone into consumption, and for four years he had been a helpless invalid, having to be fed with a spoon.

While I was up on that mountain top I was reminded of the transfiguration scene, and I felt that the Lord's only purpose in taking us into the glory was to fit us for greater usefulness in the valley. Now as I was on this mountain top that day, the Lord said to me, "I want you to go and raise Lazarus." I told the brother who accompanied me what the Lord told me, and when we got down to the valley, I wrote a postcard: “When I was up on the mountain praying today, God told me that I was to go and raise Lazarus." I addressed the postcard to the man in the place whose name had been given to me by the two lads.

When we arrived at the place we went to the man to whom I had addressed the card to. He looked at me and said, "Did you send this?" I said, "Yes." He said, "Do you think we believe in this? Here, take it." And he threw it at me.

The man called a servant and said, "Take this man and show him Lazarus." Then he said to me, "The moment you see him you will be ready to go home. Nothing will keep you here then." Everything he said was true from the natural viewpoint. The man was completely helpless. He was nothing but a mass of bones with skin stretched over them. There was no life to be seen at all. Everything in him spoke of decay and death.

I said to him, "Will you shout? You remember that at Jericho the people shouted while the walls were still up. God has the same type of victory for you if you will only believe." But I could not get him to believe not even an ounce. There was not an atom of faith in his heart. He had decided in his mind that there was no hope.

It is a blessed thing to learn that God's word can never fail. Never hearken to human plans or ideals. God can work mightily when you persist in believing Him in spite of discouragements from the human standpoint. When I got back to the man to whom I had sent the post-card, he asked, "Are you ready to go now?"

I told him I am not moved by what I see. I am moved only by what I believe. I know this for a fact that no man who was walking by faith looks at the circumstances if he believes. No man considers how he feels if he believes. The man who believes God has victory in every situation. Every man who comes into the fullness of the spirit can laugh at all things and believe God. There is something in the full gospel work that is different from anything else in the world. Somehow, in Pentecost, you know that God is a reality. Wherever the Holy Ghost has His way, the gifts of the Spirit will be in manifestation; and where these gifts are never in manifestation, I question whether He is present. Holy Ghost people are spoiled for anything else than Holy Ghost meetings. We want none of the entertainments that the churches are offering. When God comes in He entertains us Himself. Entertained by the King of kings and Lord of lords! O, it is wonderful.

There were spiritually difficult conditions in that Welsh village, and it seemed impossible to get the people to believe. "Ready to go home?" I was asked. But a man and a woman there asked us to come and stay with them. I said, "I want to know how many of you people can pray." No one wanted to pray. I asked if I could get seven people to pray with me for the poor man's deliverance. I said to the two people who were going to entertain us, "I will count on you two, and there is my friend and myself, and we need three others." I told the people that I trusted that some of them would awaken to their responsibility and come in the morning and join us in prayer for the raising of Lazarus. It will never do to give way to human opinions. If God says a thing, you are to believe it. Never even asked people what they think, because all the abundance of their heart they will utter their unbelief.

I told the people that I would not eat anything that night. When I went to bed it seemed as if the devil tried to place on me everything that he had placed on that poor man in the bed. When I awoke I had a cough and all the weakness of a tubercular patient. I rolled out of bed on to the floor and cried out to God to deliver me from the power of the devil. I shouted loud enough to wake everybody in the house, but nobody was disturbed. God gave me wonderful victory, and I got back into bed again as free as ever I was in my life. At 5 o'clock the Lord awakened me and said to me, "Don't break bread until you break it round my table." At 6 o'clock He gave me these words, "And I will raise him up." I put my elbow into the fellow who was sleeping with me. He said, "Ugh!" I put my elbow into him again and said, "Do you hear? The Lord says that He will raise Lazarus up."

At 8 o'clock they said to me, "Have a little refreshment." But I have found prayer and fasting the greatest joy, and you will always find it so when you are led by God. When we went to the house where Lazarus lived there were eight of us altogether. No one can prove to me that God does not always answer prayer. He always does more than we ask or think. He always gives exceedingly abundant above all we ask or think.

I shall never forget how the power of God fell on us as we went into that sick man's room. O, it was lovely! As we circled round the bed I got one brother to hold one of the sick man's hands and I held the other; and we each held the hand of the person next to us. I said, "We are not going to pray, we are just going to use the name of Jesus." We all knelt down and whispered that one word, "Jesus! Jesus! Jesus!" The power of God fell and then it lifted. Five times the power of God fell and then it remained. But the person who was in the bed was unmoved. Two years previous someone had come along and had tried to raise him up, and the devil had used his lack of success as a means of discouraging him. I said, "I don't care what the devil says; if God says he will raise you up it must be so. Forget everything else except what God says about Jesus."

The sixth time the power fell and the sick man's lips began moving and the tears began to fall. I said to him, "The power of God is here; it is yours to accept it." He said, "I have been bitter in my heart, and I know I have grieved the Spirit of God. Here I am helpless. I cannot lift my hands, nor even lift a spoon to my mouth." I said, "Repent, and God will hear you." He repented and cried out, "O God, let this be to Thy glory." As he said this the virtue of the Lord went right through him.

I have asked the Lord to never let me tell this story except as it was, for I realize that God cannot bless exaggerations. As we again said, "Jesus! Jesus! Jesus!" the bed shook, and the man shook. I said to the people that were with me, "You can all go down stairs right away. This is all God. I'm not going to assist him." I sat and watched that man get up and dress himself. We sang the doxology as he walked down the steps. I said to him, "Now tell what has happened."

It was soon noised abroad that Lazarus had been raised up from the bed of death and the people came from Llanelly and all the district around to see him and hear his testimony. God brought salvation to many. This man preached right out in the open air what God had done, and as a result many were convicted and converted. All this came through the name of Jesus, through faith in His name, yea, the faith that is by Him gave this sick man perfect soundness in the presence of them all.

.

# CHAPTER FIVE

**Smith - Jesus bore my sins and sicknesses. If I dare believe, then I am justified. If I dare believe, then I am healed.**

#126 We had a meeting in Stockholm that I shall ever bear in mind. There was a home for incurables there and one of the inmates was brought to the meeting. He had palsy and was shaking all over. He stood up before 3,000 people and came to the platform, supported by two others. The power of God fell on him as I anointed him in the name of Jesus.

The moment I touched him he dropped his crutch and began to walk in the name of Jesus. He walked down the steps and round that great building in view of all the people. There is nothing that our God cannot do. He will do everything if you will dare to believe. Someone said to me, "Will you go to this Home for Incurables?" They took me there on my rest day. They brought out the sick people into a great corridor and in one hour the Lord set about twenty of them free. The name of Jesus is so marvelous.

**#128** There are many that say they are believers but they are full of sickness and do not take a hold of the life of the Lord Jesus Christ that is provided for them. I was taken to see a woman who was dying and said to her, "How are you doing spiritually?"

She answered, "I have faith, I believe." I said, "You know that you do not have faith, you know that you are dying. It is not faith that you have, it is mere mental acknowledgment." There is a difference between knowing something in your head and having faith. I saw that she was in the influence of the devil. There was no possibility of divine life until the enemy was removed from the premises.

I hate the devil, and I laid hold of the woman and shouted, "Come out, you devil of death. I command you to come out in the name of Jesus." In one minute she stood on her feet in completely healed and in victory.

**#129** I was at a camp meeting in Cazadero, California, several years ago, and a remarkable thing happened. A man came to the meeting who was stone deaf. I prayed for him and I knew that God had healed him. Then came the test.

He would always move his chair up to the platform, and every time I got up to speak he would get up as close as he could and strain his ears to catch what I had to say. The devil said, "It isn't done." I declared, "It is done." This went on for three weeks and then the manifestation came and he could hear distinctly up to sixty yards away.

When his ears were opened he thought it was so great that he had to stop the meeting and tell everybody about it. I met him in

Oakland recently and he was hearing perfectly. As we remain steadfast and unmovable on the ground of faith, we shall see what we believe for in perfect manifestation.

**#133** I had been preaching at Stavanger in Norway, and was very tired and wanted a few hours rest. I went to my next appointment, arriving at about 9:30 in the morning. My first meeting was to be at night. I said to my interpreter, "After we have had something to eat, let us go down to the fjords." We spent three or four hours down by the sea and at about 4:30 returned.

We found the end of the street, which has a narrow entrance, just filled with autos, wagons, etc., containing invalids and sick people of every kind. I went up to the house and was told that the house was full of sick people. It reminded me of the scene described in the fifth chapter of Acts. I began praying for the people in the street and God began to heal the people. How wonderfully He healed those people who were in the house. We sat down for a lunch and the telephone bell rang and someone at the other end was saying, "What shall we do? The town hall is already full; the police cannot control things."

In that little Norwegian town the people were jammed together, and oh, how the power of God fell upon us. A cry went up from every one, "Is this the revival?"

Revival is coming. The breath of the Almighty is coming. The breath of God shows up every defect, and as it comes flowing in like a river, everybody will need a fresh anointing, a fresh cleansing of the blood. You can depend upon it that that breath is upon us.

**#134** At one time I was at a meeting in Ireland. There were many sick carried to that meeting and helpless ones were helped there. There were many people in that place who were seeking for the Baptism of the Holy Ghost. Some of them had been seeking for years. There were sinners there who were under mighty conviction. There came a moment when the breath of God swept through the meeting. In about ten minutes every sinner in the place was saved. Everyone who had been seeking the Holy Spirit was baptized, and every sick one was healed. God is a reality and His power can never fail. As our faith reaches out, God will meet us and the same rain will fall. It is the same blood that cleanses, the same power, the same Holy Ghost, and the same Jesus made real through the power of the Holy Ghost. What would happen if we should believe God?

**Smith - Many want to be healed, but harbor things in their hearts. Let these things go. Forgive, and the Lord will forgive you.**

**#135** I was passing through the city of London one time, and Mr. Mundell, the secretary of the Pentecostal Missionary Union, learned that I was there. He arranged for me to meet him at a certain place at 3:30 p. m. I was to meet a certain boy whose father and mother lived in the city of Salisbury. They had sent this young man to London to take care of their business. He had been a leader in Sunday school work but he had been betrayed and had fallen. Sin is awful and the wages of sin is death. But there is another side-the gift of God is eternal life.

This young man was in great distress; he had contracted a horrible disease and feared to tell anyone. There was nothing but death ahead for him. When the father and mother got to know of his condition they suffered inexpressible grief.

When we got to the house, Brother Mundell suggested, that we get down to prayer. I said, "God does not say so, we are not going to pray yet. I want to quote a scripture, ***`Fools, because of their transgression, and because of their iniquities, are afflicted: their soul abhorreth all manner of meat; and they draw near unto the***

***gates of death.'"*** The young man cried out, "I am that fool." He broke down and told us the story of his fall. Oh, if men would only repent, and confess their sins, how God would stretch out His hand to heal and to save. The moment that young man repented, a great abscess burst, and God sent virtue into his life, giving him a mighty deliverance and he was completely healed of that terrible disease.

**#137** At a meeting I was holding, the Lord was working and many were being healed. A man saw what was taking place and remarked, "I'd like to try this thing." He came up for prayer and told me that his body was broken in two places. I laid my hands on him in the name of the Lord, and said to him, "Now, you believe God."

The next night he was at meeting and he got up like a lion. He said, "I want to tell you people that this man here is deceiving you. He laid his hands on me last night for a rupture in two places, but I'm not a bit better." I stopped him and said, "You are healed, your trouble is that you won't believe it."

He was at meeting the next night and when there was opportunity for testimony this man arose. He said, "I'm a mason by trade. Today I was working with a laborer and he had to put a big stone in place. I helped him and did not feel any pain. I said to myself, `How can this be possible?' I went away to a place where I could strip, and found that I was healed." I told the people, "Last night this man was not of God, but now I know I was completely wrong.

**#140** I went to a house one afternoon where I had been called, and met a man at the door. He said, "My wife has not been out of bed for eight months; she is completely paralyzed. She has been looking so much for you to come, she is hoping God will raise her up." I went in and rebuked the devil's power. She said, "I know I am healed; if you go out I will get up."

I left the house, and went away not hearing anything more about her situation. I went to a meeting that night, and a man jumped up and said he had something he wanted to say; he had to go to catch a train but wanted to talk first. He said, "I come to this city once a week, and I visit the sick all over the city.

There is a woman I have been visiting and I was very much in despair about her; she was completely paralyzed and has laid on that bed many months, and when I went there today she was up doing her work." I tell this story because I want you to see Jesus.

**Wilt Thou Be Made Whole?**

**#141** I visited a woman who had been suffering for many years. She was all twisted up with rheumatism and had been two years in this condition in bed. I said to her, "why are you laying here in this condition as a believer?" She said, "I've come to the conclusion that I have a thorn in the flesh."

I said, "To what wonderful degree of righteousness or revelation have you attained that you have to have a thorn in the flesh? Have you had such an abundance of divine revelations that there is danger of your being exalted above measure ?" She said, "I believe it is the Lord who is causing me to suffer." I said, "You believe it is the Lord's will for you to suffer, and yet you are trying to get out God's will as quickly as you can. Look there are doctor's bottles all over the place.

It is time to get off your high and holy place and confess that you are a sinner. If you'll get rid of your self-righteousness, God will do something for you. Drop the idea that you are so holy that God has got to afflict you. Sin is the cause of your sickness and not righteousness. Disease is not caused by righteousness, but by sin."

There is healing through the blood of Christ and deliverance for every captive. God never intended His children to live in misery because of some affliction that comes directly from the devil. A perfect atonement was made at Calvary. I believe that Jesus bore my sins, and I am free from them all. I am justified from all things if I dare believe. He Himself took our infirmities and bare our sicknesses; and if I dare believe, I can be healed.

**#142** I was in Long Beach, California, one day, with a friend, we were passing a hotel. He told me of a doctor there who had a diseased leg; that he had been suffering from it for six years, and could not get out. We went up to his room and found four doctors there. I said, "Well, doctor, I see you have plenty of help, I'll call again another day."

I was passing that same hotel another time, and the Spirit said, "Go join thyself to him." Poor doctor! He surely was in a bad condition. He said, "I have been like this for six years, and nothing human can help me." I said, "You need God Almighty." People are trying to patch up their lives; but you cannot do anything without God. I talked to him for a while about the Lord, and then prayed for him. I cried, "Come out of him, in the name of Jesus." The doctor cried, "It's all gone!"

I was in Long Beach about six weeks later, and the sick were coming for prayer. Among those filling up the aisle was the doctor. I said, "What is the trouble now?" He said, "Diabetes, but it will be all right tonight. I know it will be all right.

At that meeting there was an old man helping his son to the altar. He said, "He has many seizures every day." Then there was a woman with a cancer. Oh, what sin has done! We read that, when God brought forth His people from Egypt, "there was not one feeble person among their tribes" (Ps. 105:37). No disease! All healed by the power of God! I believe that God wants a people like that today. All of these precious people including that Doctor was healed.

**#143** A young woman declares: "I was brought to last Sunday's meeting a poor, dying woman, with a disease which was eating into every part of my being. I was full of corruption outside as well as in; but the Lord Jesus Christ came and loosed me and set me free. Since then I have slept better and have eaten more heartily than I have for eight years."

*The president of the Methodist Local Preachers' Association testified to having been delivered from nervous trouble.

**#145** A lady said: "While sitting in in one of Mister Wigglesworth services, listening to the Word, God healed me of liver trouble, gall stones and sciatica. He has also touched my daughter who was suffering with her feet, having been operated on twice; she had little hope of being anything but an invalid the rest of her life; but the Lord operated. All pain has gone. She is no longer an invalid. Praise the Lord."

**#146** Mr. Lewellyn, a Church of England "Reader," testified to having been immediately healed of a stiff knee.

*Mr. Barrett testified that Miss Witt, of Box Hill, who has been 22 years in an invalid chair, rose and walked after Mr. Wigglesworth ministered to her in the name of Jesus.

*Another testified of having been healed the night before of rheumatoid arthritis of four years standing, discarding crutch and stick.

*Mr. Johnsone of Sperm Vale, who had been deaf twenty years, and his wife, who had sat in a wheelchair for six years, were immediately healed. The empty chair was wheeled to the railway station, the woman testifying to passersby of the great things God had done for her.

**#147** I prayed for a sister who had cancer and she said, "I know I'm free and that God has delivered me." Then they brought the boy with the seizures, and I commanded the evil spirits to leave, in the name of Jesus.

Then I prayed for the doctor. At the next night's meeting the house was full. I called out, "Now, doctor, what about the diabetes?" He said, "It has gone." Then I said to the old man, "What about your son?" He said, "He hasn't had any fits since." We have a God who answers prayer.

**#148** "I slipped and fell on Broadway, San Diego, in February, 1921 I discovered afterwards that I had fractured the base of my spine. I had so severely wrenched the hips and pelvic bones that I was filled with great pain from that moment forward. As the broken bone was not discovered and set until about two months after the accident, the constant pain and irritation caused a general inflammation of my nervous system, and the long delay in getting the bone set, made it impossible to heal, so that, my condition steadily grew worse.

I was taken to the hospital and the bone was removed about a month after it had been set. Though the wound healed rapidly, the nervous inflammation remained, and so for many months longer I was in constant pain and unable to get around without assistance. I was taken to the first service held by Mr. Wigglesworth on the 2nd of October, 1922. At the close of the service all those who were sick and in pain and had come for healing were requested to rise if possible. My husband assisted me to my feet, and as those were prayed for by Mister Wigglesworth in the name of Jesus Christ I was instantly healed. How I was healed I do not know. I only know the Great Physician touched my body and I was made whole, and freed from pain.

"After I got home I showed everyone how I could sit down and rise with my hands above my head; when before it had taken both hands to push up my feeble body, and I had to have straps on my bed to pull myself up by. No more use for them now! I lay down and turned over for the first time since the accident without pain. I shall never cease to praise God for the healing of my body through the precious blood of Jesus and in His name. I walked to the street car alone the next day and attended the next service and have been "on the go" ever since. To Jesus be all the, praise and glory." – Mrs. Sanders, 4051 Bay View Court, San Diego, Calif.

**#149** One day Smith and his wife received a letter from a young man asking for prayer. He had been healed about three years before of a bad foot, and they had lost all trace of him since, until this urgent cry came from a home where in the natural, death was soon to enter. When the letter came Mrs. Wigglesworth said to her husband, "If you go, God will give you this case."

He telegraphed back that he would go. Wigglesworth got on his bicycle riding from Grantham, nine miles away to Willsford. When he reached the village he inquired where the young man, Matthew Snell, lived. This young man had heart failure and had to lie perfectly still in one place. The doctor said if he moved from that place he would surely die, and left him, never expecting to see him alive again. When Mr. Wigglesworth reached the house, the mother of the young man stood in the doorway and said, "Oh you have come too late." "Is he alive at all?" He asked the mother. "Yes, he is just barely alive."

Smith went into the parlor where he was lying. The young man, Matthew, said in a barely audible voice, "I cannot rise, I am too weak, and the doctor says if I turn around I shall die." Mr. Wigglesworth said this to him, "Matthew, the Lord is the strength of your heart and thy portion altogether. Will you believe that the Lord will raise you up for His glory?" The young man answered, "Lord, if You will raise me up for Your glory I will give You my life." Hands were laid on him in the name of the Lord Jesus Christ and instantly new life came into him.

"Shall I arise?" he asked, but Wigglesworth felt in his heart that the young man should lie perfectly quiet and so advised. The night was spent in prayer and the next morning Brother Wigglesworth attended the ten o'clock meeting in the Primitive Methodist Chapel. He was asked to speak and talked of faith in God, and from that moment the unbelief seemed to clear away from the village people. They came to him at the close of the service and said, "We believe Matthew will be raised up."

He had asked the family to air Matthew's clothing for him for that he could wear them, but they did not do it because they did not believe he would be healed. For six weeks he had been in a very serious condition, becoming weaker all the time. Mr. Wigglesworth strongly insisted on them preparing Matthew's clothes. They finally relented not because they believed for healing, but to satisfy him. About 2:30 he went into the room where the young man lay and said,

"Now I would like this to be for the glory of God. It shall never be said that Wigglesworth raised you up." The young man answered, "For Thy glory, Lord; my life shall be for Thee." Then the servant of the Lord said, "Matthew, I believe the moment I lay hands on you the glory of God will fill this place so I shall not be able to stand." As he did this the glory of the Lord fell upon them until he fell on his face to the floor; it increased until everything in the room shook, the bed and Matthew who was on the bed, and with a strong voice the young man cried out, "For Thy glory, Lord !" "For Thy glory!"

This continued for at least fifteen minutes, when it was apparent to them God would give him strength not only to rise but to dress in the glorious power which seemed like the description given of the temple being filled with the glory of God, and the young man was walking up and down, shouting and praising God and clapping his hands.

He went to the door and called to his father that the Lord had raised him up. His father was a backslider and fell down before God and cried for mercy. His sister, who had been brought out of an asylum and was threatened with another attack of insanity, in the manifestation of that glory was delivered from that time. That weak body immediately became strong, eating regular food immediately. The doctor came and examined his heart and declared it was all right. Matthew declared it should be for the Lord's glory and at once began preaching in the power of the Holy Ghost. His own statement is that when he gives the story of his healing many are saved.

**#151** A friend of Smith's was dying. They had been kindred spirits from their boyhood days, perfect love existed between them. When Mr. Wigglesworth reached home one evening he found his wife had gone to see his friend who was sick and he immediately started down to see him also.

As he neared the house he knew something serious had happened, and as he passed up the stairway he found the wife of the sick man lying on the stairs, broken-hearted. Death had already taken place. As he entered the room where the man lay, the deep love he had always cherished overcame him and he lost control of himself and began crying out to God.

His wife who was present tried to constrain him, but as his heart went out to God he was lost to all around and felt he was being drawn up by the Spirit into the heavenlier. The deep cry of his heart was: "Father, Father, in Jesus' Name bring him back." He opened his eyes to find out there were no altered conditions, but with a living faith he cried out, "He lives! He lives! Look! Look!" The dead man opened his eyes and revived, and he is living still to the writing of this story.

.

# CHAPTER SIX

**#152** A young woman came into Smith's mission one night and was so impressed with what she heard that at the close she said to Mrs. Wigglesworth: "There is a young woman at Allerton who has been living there for six years and never been outside the door. Will you go up there?" Mrs. Wigglesworth referred her to her husband and he said he would go.

As he started down the road, which was filled with people traveling to and fro, the Holy Ghost fell upon him so that he stood in the street and shouted for joy, and the tears rained down his face and saturated his waistcoat. To his astonishment, nobody in the street seemed to recognize his condition; it seemed as though the Lord covered him. He dared not speak to anybody lest the presence of the Lord should leave him.

The young woman who went with him was full of talk, but he said nothing. As soon as he entered the house the glory of God came more fully upon him and as he lay hands on this poor afflicted woman the glory of God filled the house. He was so filled with God's glory he rushed out of the house and the young woman running after him exclaiming, "How did you get this glory? Tell me! Tell me!" He told her to go back into the house and seek the Lord.

A week after that he was in an office in Bradford and as soon as he entered the office a man said, "Wigglesworth, sit down. I want to tell you something." He sat down to listen, and the office-man said, "Last Sunday night at the chapel the preacher was in the midst of preaching when suddenly the door swung open, and in came a young woman who had been confined to her home for six years.

She stood up and said that as she came out of the house the heavens were covered with the most glorious light and presence of God, and she read over the heavens. 'The Lord is coming soon.'" Mr. Wigglesworth wept and praised God, but said nothing. He realized that God wanted him to know the young lady had been healed but that he was not to talk about it.

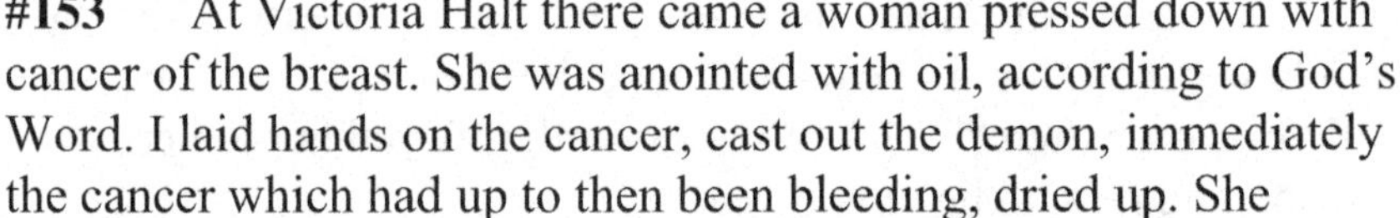

**#153** At Victoria Halt there came a woman pressed down with cancer of the breast. She was anointed with oil, according to God's Word. I laid hands on the cancer, cast out the demon, immediately the cancer which had up to then been bleeding, dried up. She received a deep impression through the Spirit that the work was done, and closely watched the healing process together with a lady friend.

The cancer began to move from its seat, and in five days dropped out entirely into the protecting bandage. They were greatly blessed and full of joy, and when looking into the cavity from whence the tumor had come, they saw to their amazement and surprise that not one drop of blood had been shed at the separation of the cancer. The cavity was sufficiently large to receive a small cup and they noticed that the sides were of a beautiful reddish hue.

During the next two days, and while they were watching

closely they saw the cavity fill up with flesh and a skin formed over it, so that at last there was only a slight scar. At two meetings this lady, filled with enthusiasm, held in her hand a glass vessel containing the cancer, and declared how great things God had done unto her.

**#155** A preacher, suffering many days from the kick of a horse, walking with great pain and in much distress, made a special call at the hotel in which I was staying, and being led by the Spirit, according to God's Word, I laid hands on the bruised ankle. A fire broke out with burning and healing power, and from that moment on he could walk easily and without pain.

**#156** A boy came to a meeting on crutches, suffering from a broken ankle. Prayer was made and hands were laid upon him, I had him to walk across the platform. He declared that he had no pain, it was all gone, and carried off his crutches under his arm.

**#157** In one of the meetings a girl came up and said she had not been able to smell for five years, and I said to her, "You will smell to-day," and in the next meeting she came to testify of being healed, and I called her on the platform, and she made a clear statement of receiving instant healing and smelling. Then at the close of that meeting one came up who had not smelt for twelve years and another for twenty years.

I said to them, "You will smell to-night." This sounds like presumption, and certainly is extravagance of language, and on the natural lines could not be understood, but God's Word has creative power, and only in faith of the Word being creative power can we ever expect to see His mighty works made manifestIn the name of Jesus I anointed, laid hands, and commanded the bound to be loosed, and instantly these two women were made to smell the oil.

The one that had been bound for twenty years was quite an inspiration by her testimony, as she imparted faith to others by saying she had more pleasure in smelling things on the table than in eating. I cannot stop to give you all the cases, but at this place there were many wonderful deliverances.

**#158** A young woman, through many operations, had parts of her hearing senses removed from the head, and asked if that would make any difference to her being made to hear, and knowing that her faith in the Word of God could recreate the defective parts, I at once ministered according to God's Word, believing that instant power would be given.

To show that there is a necessity of the one who receives to believe as well as the one who ministers to bring about God's divine plan, she left the platform as she came on apparently no different, but being in the midst of people who were constantly being definitely healed, she appeared again the second time on the platform. She said this time "I am going to believe I shall be healed," and I said, "You, will be healed before you leave the platform," and that night a miracle was performed. From that day she also was a great inspiration to those gathered.

**#160** On one occasion a woman with a cancer on her nose and upper part of her face came forward to be prayed for and he got her to stand right in front of the people and said to them, "Look at her. She will be here tomorrow night and you will see what God has done for her." He prayed and she left the meeting. The next night she attended the meeting and it was seen that the cancer had gone and there was a new skin on her face. There was another case of a young woman whose face was in a terrible condition through some disease she had contracted. She was prayed for and the next day appeared with a perfectly clean face and the new skin had a brilliant appearance.

**#161** A young man came to the meetings to ridicule, but he appeared to be struck dumb, for he could not speak. The brother commanded the demon to come out of him and his tongue was loosed. At another meeting three insane people were sent and put in the front row with a view to creating a tumult, but the brother had discernment, and in the name of Jesus commanded the demons to keep quiet and there was no further trouble. Souls were saved and bodies healed at every meeting and in many instances baptized in the Holy Ghost, with a bursting out in other tongues.

**#162** At Copenhagen, Denmark: So far, no buildings have been large enough, and hundreds have been turned away." After ministering in a hall which holds 3,000, a hall holding 5,000 was to be obtained.

Police on horseback had to control the crowds. "Only by a great squeezing could I get into the hall, assisted by the police officers." Piles of crutches were left behind, the blind saw, epileptic fits dealt with, etc…: "I am at the feet of Jesus, and weep through my address, and God breaks forth upon the people, and there are rows of people each night seeking salvation."

**#163** Bro. Wigglesworth writes: "A poor lame man in a hospital asked the doctor if he could leave to attend the meetings, but was refused permission. He was told that if he broke the regulations he would not be permitted to return.

He replied that he did not expect that he would have to return, and it was so." When Bro. Wigglesworth laid hands on him (not knowing all this) he was healed instantly, and left his crutches with the others.

**#164** I came to seek help myself, being worn out with long unbroken service in the Lord's work. I had not heard of Mr. Wigglesworth before, but I knew that Pastor Barratt, my spiritual father, was there. The next day there was a meeting for healing. After the preaching service I went forward into the other hall and I was surprised to find in a few minutes a crowd following.

The hall was soon full with a queue of hundreds of men and women patiently waiting for a touch of God through His servant, and, glory to God, we were not disappointed. As hands were laid upon me the power of God went through me in a mighty way. I was immediately well.

It was wonderful to notice, as the ministry continued, the effect upon the people as the power of the Lord came over them. Some lifted their hands, crying, "I am healed! I am healed!" Some fell on the platform overpowered by the power of the Spirit, having to be helped down. Others walked away as in a dream; others as drunk with new wine, lost to everything but God; but all had faces as transfigured with the glory of the Lord and magnifying Jesus.

A young blind girl, as she was ministered to, cried out, "Oh, how many windows there are in this hall!" During the three weeks the meetings continued the great chapel was crowded daily, multitudes being healed and many saved. The testimony meetings were wonderful. One said, "I was deaf, they prayed, and Jesus healed me." Another, "I had consumption, and I am free," and so on.

**#165** In the smaller hall, set apart for those seeking the Baptism of the Holy Ghost, I shall never forget the sight, how the people with eyes closed and hearts up-lifted to God waited. Did the Holy Spirit fall upon them? Of course He did. Here also many were healed. At another place there was a young man whose body was spoiled because of sin, but the Lord is merciful with sinners. He was anointed, and when hands were laid on, the power of God went mightily over him. He said, "I am healed," but being broken down, he cried as a little child confessing his sin; at the same moment the Lord saved him. Glory to God! He went into the large hall and testified to salvation and healing.

**#166** The hall held 1,800 people. At nearly every meeting crowds were unable to enter the building, but they waited on often hours and hours for the chance, if any left the building, to step into the place. Here a man with two crutches, his whole body shaking with palsy, is lifted on to the platform. (Behind him five or six hundred more are waiting for help.)

This man is anointed and hands laid upon him in the Name of Jesus. He is still shaking. Then he drops one crutch, and after a short time the other one. His body is still shaking, but he takes the first step out in faith! Will it be? He lifts one foot and then the other, walks round the platform. The onlookers rejoice with him. Now he walks around the auditorium. Hallelujah!

**#167** During a meeting a woman began to shout and shout. The preacher told her to be quiet, but instead she jumped up on a chair, flourishing her arms about, and crying, "I am healed! I am healed!

I had cancer in my mouth, and I was unsaved; but during, the meeting, as I listened to the word of God, the Lord has saved me and healed me of cancer in my mouth." She shouts again, "I am saved! I am saved! I am healed of cancer!" She was quite beside herself. The people laughed and cried together.

**#168** Here was another woman unable to walk, sitting on a chair as she was ministered to. Her experience was the same as hundreds of the others. She rose up, looking around, wondering if after all it was a dream.

Suddenly she laughed and said, "My leg is healed." Afterwards she said, "I am not saved," and streams of tears ran down her face. They prayed for her, and later she left the meeting healed and saved and full of joy. We have a wonderful Savior; glory to His Holy Name!

**#169** A man and his son came in a taxi to a meeting. Both had crutches. The father had been in bed two years and was unable to put his leg to the ground. He was ministered to. He dropped both crutches, walking and praising God.

When the son saw this he cried out. "Help me too," and after a little while father and son, without crutches and without taxi, walked away from the hall together. That word again is manifested; the same Jesus, the wonder-working Jesus is just the same today.

**#170** During three weeks thousands daily attended the meetings. Each morning two or three hundred were ministered to for healing. Each evening the platform was surrounded. Again and again, as each throng retired another company came forward seeking salvation. Here many were baptized in the Holy Ghost. The testimony meetings were wonderful.

Now I will close with a vision a brother had who attended these meetings. He was lost in intercession for the hundreds of sick waiting to be ministered to for healing. He saw an opening from the platform, where the sick were, right into the glory. He saw wonderful beings in the form of men resting who, with interest, looked on.

Again he looked at the platform and saw a heavenly Being clothed in white, who all the time was more active than any other in helping the sick, and when He touched them the effect was wonderful. Bent forms were made straight, their eyes shone, they began to glorify and praise the Lord. A Voice said: "Healings are the smallest of all gifts; it is but a drop in the bucket in view of what God has in store for His children. Ye shall do greater works than these."

**#171** There were many remarkable healings. Many suffering with cancer, tumors, tuberculosis, rupture, rheumatism and many other diseases have been miraculously healed through the prayer of faith.

We read of one man who was suffering with tuberculosis of the stomach who attended one of our brother's meetings in Switzerland. He was brought in a dying condition on a stretcher in a wagon. By his side was a basket of food, and a friend, knowing his condition, asked the reason for its presence. "I shall eat it going back," was his simple answer, and he did!

#**172** Our dear Brother Wigglesworth arrived in Melbourne last Thursday, February 16th, Amongst those who came forward for prayer were several who declared that they had received remarkable and instantaneous healings. A few of those were as follows: One little girl, six years of age, was seen, after prayer by the evangelist, walking out of the front door of the building with her mother, who was delightedly exclaiming to all and sundry, "Look at her!

She has never walked in her life before!" A man who had not walked for over four years owing to rheumatoid arthritis, was instantly healed, and after triumphantly passing his stick and crutch up to the platform, gave an impromptu exhibition of the power that had come into his legs by jumping and leaping and praising God.

Others suffering from weak spine, nerve and heart trouble, weak eyesight, asthma, kidney trouble, loss of voice, etc., claimed to have been wonderfully helped.

Since the first night there have been many other wonderful healings. Last night a dear woman who had been unable to walk for 61 years was brought to be prayed for, and—glory be to

God!—she got out of her chair and walked, and her husband pushed her chair along, with her walking behind. Praise our covenant-keeping God! Truly He is able to do exceeding abundantly above all that we can ask or think.

There have also been many conversions—at one meeting alone 40 dear ones accepted Jesus as their Lord and Savior—and we are believing for still greater things. The revival showers are falling and God is working. Bless His holy Name!

Just this morning a mother brought her little girl along, who had fallen on a pair of scissors, and cut her mouth so that she could not close it. After the evangelist had laid his hands upon it and prayed, she was able to close her mouth and was quite well. Glory to God!

---

**#173** At a series of meetings conducted during the last ten days by Mr. Smith Wigglesworth, a Yorkshire evangelist, there have been many "manifestations of healing." Mr. Wigglesworth held his earlier meetings in the Good News Hall, North Melbourne, and at first the attendance was only moderate; but this week it was necessary to transfer to Olympia, as so many persons had to be turned away from the smaller hall.

Last night a large number of persons came "for aid," to use the evangelist's expression; and though he was not successful in all cases, there; were many in which there appeared to be startling and immediate improvement after he had laid his; hands on the afflicted and prayed over them. In one instance a woman who was said to have been very deaf was able to answer him when he spoke to her in an ordinary tone.

In another an elderly man, who declared that he had suffered from; noises in the head for ten years, said that he was free from them at last. An elderly woman who was described as almost crippled with rheumatism, was directed to stoop down and touch the ground with her hands. "I don't suppose you have bent your back for some time," Mr. Wigglesworth said. The patient stooped down without effort! Apparently, and was so delighted that she laughed heartily. "No pain and no stiffness now?" asked the evangelist, and she replied that she had none.

A girl who had an affliction of the hip and knee, which it was said had prevented her walking without a stick for some years, walked up and down to front of the audience at a rapid pace, whereas she had only been able before to limp slowly with the aid of her stick. "Throw your stick away; burn it," said Mr. Wigglesworth. "You will not want it again." Many other cases gave interesting results.

**Smith - They think I am rather unmerciful in my dealing with the sick. No, I have no mercy for the devil.**

**#174** Further demonstrations of "healing by touch" were given by Mr. Smith Wigglesworth, a Yorkshire evangelist, before a very large assemblage at the Olympia last night. After the evangelist had given an address on the subject of "Faith," he called upon those who had come "for aid" on Tuesday night to testify as to the results; and several persons who had been suffering front deafness, rheumatics, and lameness declared that their ailments had completely gone.

Mr. Wigglesworth healing by touch." An elderly man, who said that he had been deaf for years, cried "Hallelujah! Hallelujah!" when asked by Mr. Wigglesworth if he could hear, after hands had been placed on him and he had been prayed over. A woman who, who had stiff legs for over 20 years, and who limped to Olympia on the arm of a relative, ran about the hall in joy after she had been "touched." Another woman, who was said to have been an invalid in a chair for 23 years, declared that her limbs were "beginning to move." She was advised by the evangelist to retain her faith in Jesus Christ and her cure; would be complete.

A young woman with pains of long standing "in her back was able to stoop and touch the ground with her hands, and she laughed heartily as she told the audience that her trouble had gone. A woman, who asserted that she had been unable to walk owing to pain in her feet, ran up and down in front of the audience, crying, "Praise the name of the Lord." She declared that her pain vanished when the evangelist touched her.

---

**#175** On February 16, 1922, God began His mighty work in Melbourne under the ministry of Mr. Smith Wigglesworth. Testimonies are called for in order that the faith of those who come to receive the Savior's touch may be quickened. A young woman who had been suffering with consumption declared, "I was brought to last Sunday's meeting a poor dying woman, with a disease that was eating into every part of my being. I was full of disease outside as well as in, but Jesus Christ came and loosed me and set me free. I have slept better and eaten more heartily than I have for eight years."

The President of the Methodist Local Preachers' Association testified to having been delivered from nervous trouble. A prominent businessman said, "The first night of this campaign God delivered me from an affliction of the feet I had had for fifty years, since I was two years of age. I am now fifty-two. Ever since I was prayed for I have had no pain. Friends have never seen me do this (stamping his feet). I have no further use for my stick."

A lady testified, - "As soon as I was anointed, the power of God went through me. Also my families have all been saved during these meetings." Mrs. S. said, "While sitting in my seat listening to the Word, God healed me of liver trouble, gallstone, and sciatica. He has also touched my daughter and manifested His power in her body. She was suffering with her feet and had been operated on twice, but as she sat in her seat the Lord began to operate and all pain was gone."

Mrs. B. said, "I was deaf, and suffering with anemia and with my feet, but as soon as hands were laid upon me for healing my ears were opened and I thank God for healing me and for this wonderful salvation for spirit, soul and body which I never saw before."

Mr. L., a Church of England reader, testified that he had been immediately healed of a stiff knee.

Mr. B. testified that a lady of Box Hill, who had been twenty-two years in an invalid's chair, rose and walked after Mr. Wigglesworth had ministered to her in the Name of Jesus.

Mr. V., a suburban Protestant Federation Society Secretary, testified that a friend was healed the night before of rhomboid arthritis of four years' standing, and had discarded stick and crutch. The friend rose in the audience saying, "I am the one."

Mr. J., of Spring Vale, who had been deaf for twenty years, was healed, and also his wife, who had sat in a wheel chair for six years; both were immediately healed. The empty chair was wheeled to the railway station, while the woman testified to all bystanders of the great things the Lord had done for her. Many were healed through the application of anointed handkerchiefs.

**#176** I feel I must express my deep gratitude for blessing received. Only those who have been in the furnace of affliction can realize the joy of deliverance. It seems too wonderful. After fourteen years of anguish, sleeplessness, and spiritual depression, caused by the bondage of the adversary, these are things of the past.

As Bro. Wigglesworth says, consumption is of the devil, and only the Lion of Judah could have delivered me from this dread scourge, which had made my body a mass of corruption. Hallelujah! KATHLEEN GAY.

# CHAPTER SEVEN

**#177** I was prayed for in Melbourne, and the evil spirit was commanded to come out. I had a polypus growth in my nose. It had been there eighteen years. When I came home from Melbourne the growth broke up and came away, for which I praise God. I had also it pain under my left breast which had troubled me twelve years.

I think it was leakage of the heart, as sorrow had caused it in the first place. At times I used to vomit blood. I have deliverance from that also. All praise to our wonder-working Jesus! MRS. T. SIMCOCK.

**#178** I have had liver problems all my life. When as a girl I was treated by the best doctors, but it always returned, and at times I was unable to turn in bed without help.

The last twelve months my kidneys were bad, and my legs swollen much with cramp. I had also varicose veins, with lumps larger than an egg. Now, glory to God, all has gone—disappeared—as soon as hands were laid upon me in the name of Jesus.

**#179** L. M Buchanan writes of the meetings held in Sydney: "A woman who was to have undergone an operation yesterday went to the doctor, who said that there was neither misplacement nor inflammation". When she told him the reason he said that she would soon be worse. Another who was to have undergone several operations because the work could not be done in one, testifies that she was free, and that the Lord had lengthened her leg two inches and that instead of limping she is now walking perfectly.

Another mother brought her little boy who had fits all day long. He was prayed for at the meeting and after the evangelist had gone he had a fit worse than before. The unbelievers' sarcasm was to be heard all over the building. Two days later the mother returned to say that the child had not had another fit. A little girl aged five years old, who had been stone-deaf three years, received her healing at once. The healings have been too numerous to mention and the preaching of the Word was wonderful."

At the meeting at Geelong, one testified. "I had a withered hand for 14 years. When Mr. Wigglesworth was here a month ago it was cured."

**#180** At Parkes a quarter of the population tried to get into the theatre. The preaching was wonderful and also the healings. A little girl, deaf for six years, eardrums burst and bleeding, was instantly healed.

Her brother, blind in one eye, received his sight immediately when he was prayed for. The daily papers say that no meetings on a religious line equal to these had ever been experienced in Parkes.

**#181** A teacher at Bunibank Methodist Sunday school testifies to healing of rheumatoid arthritis. "A doctor examined me in the beginning of December, 1911, and told me I would need new joints to walk. He said he would defy anyone to cure me, and although I improved in health I did not walk better.

On April 4th I went to be prayed with, and believed God would heal me. As hands were placed on my head in the name of Jesus, I felt the power of God go right through me. After the meeting I walked down three flights of stairs without a stick for the first time for sixteen years, and I have no use for a stick since.

I have always tried to impress upon the juniors the power of prayer, but I had not realized I would have to demonstrate it in my own life. After testifying in the Sunday school, I asked all who were Christians or who would became so to stand. Every teacher and every scholar stood, and so we sang the Doxology. Men of the world have told me 'It has set them thinking.' There is no evidence now that I had ever rheumatoid arthritis. Praise God!"

**#182** A dairyman had for 3 years suffered with chronic gastritis and paralysis of both legs from the hips downward and could only drag along with crutches.

He testifies, "On June 4th I attended the Town Hall. I was anointed, hands were laid on me, and Mr. Wigglesworth told me to walk. I handed him my crutches and walked home.

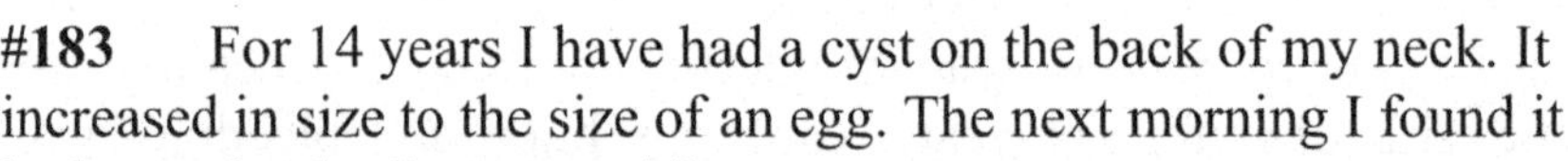

**#183** For 14 years I have had a cyst on the back of my neck. It increased in size to the size of an egg. The next morning I found it had completely disappeared."

**#184** A lady testifies, "Over 3 years ago varicose veins in my legs broke. I was twice in hospital, but when I used the legs the veins burst open. The last time they were cut and an ulcer formed. I had to walk with a stick, and could only limp.

I went to the Town Hall. I had faith that Jesus would heal me. The pain ceased and I was able to leave my stick and walk to the car. My leg is sound and the ulcer is daily healing. I am now able to wash and do my housework."

**#185** Another Wellington lady says that her son (age 11) 6 years ago broke his arm. It was badly set and he could not bend it properly. It was massaged for 12 months without any benefit. It is healed. Also her daughter, who suffered from adenoids, was healed.

**#186** A lady from Ngaio, aged 20, has suffered from double curvature of the spine from infancy. She could not walk until 4 years of age and could only rise from the floor by pulling herself up with both hands. One leg was 3 inches shorter and less in circumference.

She went to many hospitals and was sent home incurable. She states, "As soon as hands were laid upon me I was healed, my spine was straightened, in a few days my leg lengthened, and my hip, which was diseased, was healed."

**#187** For many years I suffered from bronchitis and asthma. I had pains in my chest and was very short of breath. I went to the meetings at the Olympia and Mr. Wigglesworth laid hands on me, and rebuked the evil spirit. I felt the power of God go right through me. I was immediately healed, and have not had a pain since.

**#188** I was on Feb. 4th. 1922, dressing my little girls when Thelma, aged 4, fell. I picked her up and found her bleeding at the mouth. The scissors were in her hand, and she ran the point through her lips. Her mouth began to swell, and I said. "Dear Jesus, don't let her go any further."

I hurried to the Good News Hall and the secretary carried her to Mr. Wigglesworth, who was at breakfast. In a few minutes the lady brought her back, with her mouth closed, and perfectly healed. The child told me that the gentleman had laid his hands on her lips and prayed, and that Jesus had made her better. J. M. Henderson.

**#189** I was born with a weak, crooked ankle. I was anointed at the Olympia and it was immediately straightened and made strong. I had to wear a specially formed boot and straps, these are no use to me now. I have bought ordinary boots. Medical men have attended me and could do nothing. Lily Ward.

**#190** Brother Smith Wigglesworth of England has arrived in this country after a mighty ministry A New Zealand newspaper, reporting our brother's meetings says, "Last night two hundred presented themselves for healing. Many were able to throw away crutches and sticks immediately.

Others with goiter, rheumatism, partial blindness and deafness. A woman crippled with rheumatism, walks quickly across the floor; stutterers read the Lord's prayer without stuttering. An old woman, deaf and dumb, says 'Jesus.' A man whose leg had been broken with a bad mend walks away smiling and confident without his crutches."

**#191** Wiggelsworth not only preaches the Word of God but acts it out literally; puts it into practice. To quote him, "God demands of every believer who has been baptized in the Holy Spirit that he should have some 'acts'. If you do not have them, you had better get face to face with God and demand from Him your acts."

When time was given for testimony in one of the services, people arose all over the house and testified to having been healed of many diseases: A woman healed of heart trouble, another of high blood pressure; a man of heart trouble, another of gangrene; other healings of broken arches, a sore limb of which a women had been afflicted for three years, indigestion of long standing, itching boils, lumbago, rheumatism after being afflicted thirty-eight years, insomnia, etc.

**#192** "It will rejoice your heart to hear the beautiful testimonies which are still coming in from those who were helped and blest in your meetings here in Australia. The dear people do not forget those beautiful spiritual feasts they had every morning. Do you remember that dear woman in J,---- who was too ill to be brought in the church?

She was put in the vestry, had to be carried in, was wrapped up in bandages. Well, she is now a living miracle, is going around doing her own work as well as anyone. It was a Baptist minister who brought this woman and he is now seeking to be filled with the Holy Ghost.

**#193** "Brother F. was telling us of a dear ten year old boy who did not develop; he was born deficient. As you prayed with him, he felt something go out of him and he is now perfectly delivered, and is as intelligent as any boy.

Another lady was suffering with chronic asthma and was so ill, especially at night. You prayed for her and she is now perfectly healed. These are lasting cases for which we give God the glory.

**#194** "Not many weeks ago a lady who is a professor of music, in one of your meetings was suffering with a severe pain at the back of her neck and in her nerves. As she sat in her seat and heard you give forth the precious Word of God, she called on the Name of the Lord and was perfectly healed.

She has not had any return of the trouble. An old lady who was wonderfully healed by the Lord is going around as happy as can be. She could scarcely walk about the streets, now is as nimble as a child. It is beautiful to see her. You will probably remember the family in which you were used of the Lord in bringing husband and wife together. God continues to bless that family, and now four of them have received the baptism of the Holy Spirit according to Acts 2:4."

**#195** The campaign began March 5th in a hall capable of holding a thousand people. From the first night it was a great success, hundreds being saved.

Not a night passed without many standing up and reaching out their hands to heaven, calling out, "Jesus save me! Jesus deliver me!" Each night the evangelist would single out people in the audience who were in pain, and would pray for them.

Immediately after prayer was offered the suffering ones would testify that they were free, from pain. If it was a case of stiff limbs, they were made to exercise them by walking up and down, running, stamping their feet, or waving their arms about in order to test whether the pain had actually gone.

**#196** One night a woman came up the aisle, walking in pain, her body all doubled up, and she finally fell on the floor in front of the platform, the pain was so great that Brother Wigglesworth jumped off the platform and put his hands upon her, and said, "In the name of Jesus I bind this pain and loose this woman."

Immediately she ran up and down the aisle, free from pain, and then went and sat down to listen to the message. She was perfectly whole. This demonstration had a great effect upon the crowd.

**#197** Some nights the evangelist prayed for over five hundred people, many of them coming hundreds of miles bringing their sick with them - the blind, deaf, dumb, lame, palsied, consumptive, eaten up with cancer, tumor's, epilepsy, weak-minded, deranged, crippled. God worked mighty miracles; blind eyes were opened, deaf ears unstopped, stammering tongues spoke, men on crutches put them over their shoulder and went away, stiff joints were made supple, headaches and fevers vanished, asthma was treated as an evil power and cast it out in the name of Jesus.

**#198** Handkerchiefs were brought in an ever-increasing number and piled high upon the platform. So many were brought (quite 500 some nights) that a fairly large suitcase was necessary to hold them all. One night, while our attention was diverted, a boy stole six new handkerchiefs that had been brought.

Two nights later he came back with them confessing that he had not been able to sleep since he had taken them. Many wonderful cures were wrought through this means. One was taken to a sanatorium and placed on a consumptive boy. The boy is wonderfully better, is putting on flesh and looking healthy.

**#199** Many people were helped by rising from their seats in faith and saying, "Jesus heal me," without the prayers of the evangelist at all. One woman, who had eruptions on her arms and burning sensations caused by these eruptions, was healed as she sat in her seat. Truly these were wonderful days. God's Spirit was poured out and Jesus was glorified.

**#200** The follow-on meetings have been wonderfully blessed. One woman in the Sunday morning meeting, after Brother Wigglesworth had left, was healed of three diseases. She came on the following Wednesday bringing fifteen friends with her, eleven of whom were saved that night as we gave the altar call.

I had the job of immersing eight in water while Brother Wigglesworth was here. The youngest being a Singhalese girl, seven years old. She had a wonderful testimony, and on the morning of her baptism, she had a vision of Jesus. It was a joy to my soul to take her in my arms and bury her with Christ in the water.

**#201** As a testimony of the efficiency of prayer in healing sicknesses, Mrs. Spelder of Kandy, who suffered from a virulent cancer in the stomach and whose case was abandoned as hopeless by scientific medical men, on Tuesday confessed to having been completely freed of the disease by Mr. Wigglesworth's prayer.

People of all sorts, of all ages and classes, of diverse religions and professions, have attended Mr. Wigglesworth's meetings, and though there have been scoffers among them nearly all of them have gone away impressed by his words and his actions.

**#202** Mr. Wigglesworth prays, the ailments ranging from headaches and pains in the body to rheumatism, catarrh, blindness, deafness, etc. Not a few children are brought by doting mothers and women of advanced age by loving relatives, and if their derangements are not set a right on the first day they come again and yet again.

Confirmed drunkards and smokers have been purged of the desire for intoxicants, and persons suffering from consumption and diseases due to dissolute lives have admitted to have been cured by Mr. Wigglesworth's prayer and their own.

Many prominent people have been attracted to the hall, from which none could go away without a profound impression of Mr. Wigglesworth – his deep voice, his simple but weighty words, his remarkable personality, and above all the perfect confidence of his actions, as when he says "In the name of Jesus, come out of this woman," addressing the evil spirit possessing the patient before him. "Are you healed?" he asks, and if the reply is in the affirmative, "Praise the Lord" he adds.

**#203** A lady resident in Kandy was brought down to Colombo about two weeks ago. She was suffering from cancer and was in "extremis," and the doctors in Kandy had given up all hopes. Eminent physicians consulted in Colombo were also of the same opinion.

The day Evangelist Wigglesworth arrived the relatives of the lady called on him, at the Glad Tidings Hall at Borella, and asked him to see the patient. As he was unable to go on that same day he gave them a piece of cloth, which he blessed, to be placed on the seat of the trouble pending his arrival on the next day. Immediately the cloth was placed on the patient, she said she felt relief and that the agony she was suffering for weeks and the spasms of pain left her.

The Evangelist saw her the next day and cast out what he termed the "evil spirit that was afflicting her in the form of a cancer," and the lady is today perfectly well and able to get about. She is to testify at tonight's meeting conducted by Smith Wigglesworth.

**#204** The campaign began in a large hall capable of holding a thousand people. From the first night it was a great success, hundreds were saved, not a night passing by without many standing up in response to the appeals of the Evangelist stretching their hands up to heaven, calling out, "Jesus save me, Jesus deliver me."

Then, as they stood up, the Evangelist would pray, asking the Lord to have mercy upon them and save them; then the whole audience would sing, "I do believe, I will believe, that Jesus died for me, that on the Cross, He shed His blood, for sin to set me free." Every night he would single out people in the audience, who were in pain and pray for them, and immediately after prayer was offered the suffering one would testify that they were free from pain.

If it was a case of stiff limbs, they were made to exercise them by walking up and down, running, stamping their feet, or waving their arms about in order to test whether the pain had actually gone or not.

**#205** One night a woman came up the aisle walking in pain, her body all doubled up, and she finally fell on the floor in front of the platform, the pain was so great.

Mr. Wigglesworth jumped off the platform and put his hands upon her and said, in the Name of Jesus Christ, I bind this pain and loose this woman, and she immediately ran up and down the aisle free from pain, and then went and sat down to listen to the message perfectly whole. This demonstration had a great effect upon the crowd.

**#206** Some nights the Evangelist had to pray for over five hundred people. Many of them coming hundreds of miles, bringing their sick with them – the blind, deaf, dumb, lame, paralyzed, consumptive, eaten up with cancer, tumor's, epilepsy, weak-minded, deranged, crippled, with rheumatism and many other kinds of diseases.

They came an increasing multitude, and God worked mighty miracles. Blind eyes being opened, deaf ears were unstopped, stammering tongues spoke plain, men on crutches put them over their shoulders and went away, stiff joints were made supple, headaches and fevers vanished, asthma was cursed as an evil power and cast out in the Name of Jesus.

It was a wonderful sight to see them coming, and to know that those who had faith, went away rejoicing, in a Living, Loving, Tender-hearted Savior, who had delivered them from the power of the devil that had bound them for weeks and months, and years, or a lifetime.

We know that many wonderful cures have been wrought in this way, eruptions have vanished, and a case of insanity was wonderfully helped. The father brought a handkerchief for his son in the asylum; after it had been prayed over it was taken to the asylum, placed on the son's head, and he at once began to speak like a normal being. Another one was taken to a sanatorium, and placed on a consumptive boy; the message brought from the sanatorium says the boy is wonderfully better, putting on flesh and looking healthy. Drunkard's lives have been changed by these means, desires for gambling have gone, and many wonderful deliverances have taken place. Glory to Jesus.

## TEACHING FROM SMITH WIGGLESWORTH

### *God Is Looking for Those Who Are Desperate For HIM!

God is looking, God is wanting men and women who are willing to submit, and SUBMIT, and SUBMIT, and yield, and YIELD, and YIELD to the Holy Spirit until their bodies are saturated and soaked through and through with God, until you realize that God your Father has you in such condition that at any moment He can reveal His will to you and communicate whatever He wants to say to you.

God wants us to be in a place where the least breath of heaven makes us all on fire, ready for everything. You say, "How can I have that?" Oh, you can have that as easy as anything. "Can I?" Yes, it is as simple as possible. "How?" Let heaven come in; let the Holy Ghost take possession of you.

When He comes into your body you will find out that that is the keynote of the spirit of joy and the spirit of rapture, and if you will allow the Holy Ghost to have full control you will find you are living in the Spirit, and you will find out that the opportunities will be God's opportunities, and there is a difference between God's opportunities and ours. You will find you have come to the right place at the right time, and you will speak the right word at the right time and in the right place, and you will not go a warfare at your own charge.

### * Some times when you pray for the sick you have to get rough.

But you are not dealing with a person, you are dealing with the Satanic forces that are binding the person. Your heart is full of love and compassion to all, but you are moved to a holy anger as you see the place the devil has taken in the body of the sick one, and you deal with his position with a real forcefulness.

One day a pet dog followed a lady out of her house and ran all around her feet. She said to the dog, "My dear, I cannot have you with me today." The dog wagged its tail and made a big fuss. She said, "Go home, my dear." But the dog did not go. At last she shouted roughly, "Go home," and off it went. Some people deal with the devil like that. The devil can stand all the comfort you like to give him. Cast him out!

You are dealing not with the person, you are dealing with the devil. Demon power must be dislodged in the name of the Lord: You are always right when you dare to deal with sickness as with the devil. Much sickness is caused by some misconduct, there is something wrong, there is some neglect somewhere, and Satan has had a chance to get in. It is necessary to repent and confess where you have given place to the devil, and then he can be dealt with.

# CHAPTER EIGHT

## Divine life and divine health

The Lord Jesus came to bring back to us what was forfeited in the Garden. Adam and Eve were there. And they were free from sin and disease until the first sin came, then disease, and then death came. People want to say it is not so! But I tell you, "Get the Devil out of you, and you will have a different body. Get disease out, and you will get the Devil out."

Jesus rebuked sickness, and it went, and so I want to bring you to a place where you will see that you are healed. You must give God your life; you must see that sickness has to go and God has to come in; that your lives have to be clean, and God will keep you holy; that you have to walk before God, and He will make you perfect, for God says, **"Without holiness no man shall see Him,"** and **As we walk in the light, as He is in the light, we have fellowship one with another, and the blood of Jesus Christ, God's Son, cleanses us from all sin.**

I want to say to you believers that there is a very blessed place for you to attain to, and the place where God wants you is a place of victory. When the Spirit of the Lord comes into your life there should be victory. The disciples, before they received the Holy Ghost, were always in bondage.

Jesus said to them one day, just before the Crucifixion**, "One of you shall betray Me,"** and they were so conscious of their inability and their human depravity and helplessness that they said one to another, **"Is it I?"** And then Peter was ashamed that he had taken that stand, and he rose up and said, **"Though all men deny Thee, yet will not I."** And likewise the others rose and declared that neither would they; but they, everyone did leave Him.

But, beloved, after they received the power of the enduement of the Holy Ghost upon them, if you remember, they were made like lions and met every difficulty. They were made to stand any test, and these men that failed before the Crucifixion, when the power of God fell upon them in the upper room, they spoke boldly to all those people who were gathered together and accused them of crucifying the Lord of Glory. They were bold.

What had made them so? I will tell you. **Purity is bold**. Take, for instance, a little child. It will gaze straight into your eyes for as long as you like, without winking once. The more pure, the bolder you will be. And I tell you God wants to bring us into that **Divine purity of heart and** life in order that holy boldness will possess us. Not officiousness; not swelled headedness or pride; not self-righteousness; but a pure, holy, Divine appointment by One Who will come in and live with you, defying the powers of satin, and put you in a place of victory in overcoming the world the flesh and the devil.

You can never inherited this kind of life from the flesh. That is a gift of God, by the Spirit, to all who obey. And so, none can say they wish they were overcomers, but that they have failed and failed until they have no hope. Brother, God can make YOU an overcomer. When the Spirit of God comes into your body He will transform you, He will quicken you. Oh, there is a life in the Spirit which makes you free from the law of sin and death, and there is an audacity about it and also there is a personality about it. It is the personality of the Deity of Jesus Christ. It is God in you.

I tell you that God is able to so transform and change and bring you into this new place by the Spirit that you become a new creation after God's order. There is no such thing as defeat for the believer. Without the Cross, without Christ's righteousness, without the new birth, without the indwelling Christ, without this Divine incoming of God, I will be a complete failure. But God, the Holy Ghost, can come in until we are renewed in righteousness and made the children of God. Nay, verily, the Sons of God.

Do you think that God created to make you to be a failure? God has never made man to be a failure. He made man to be a **"Son";** to walk about the earth in power; and so when I look at you I know that there is a capability that can be put into you which has the capacity of controlling and bringing everything into subjection to Christ. Yes, there is the capacity of the power of Christ to dwell in you, to put every evil thing under your feet. And you will be master over the flesh and the devil; till within you there is nothing that rises up except that which will magnify and glorify the Lord.

God wants me to show you to experience what his disciples did, who were so frail, like you and me, that we, too, may now be filled with God, and become partakers of this wonderful truth I am preaching. Here we see Peter, frail, helpless, and, at every turn of the tide, a failure. But God filled that man with the Spirit of His righteousness, till he went up and down, bold as a lion, and when he came to death, even the crucifixion space he counted himself unworthy of being crucified like his Lord, and asked that his murderers would put him head downwards on the tree. There was a deep submissiveness, and a power that was greater than all flesh. Peter had then changed by the power of God.

The Scriptures do not tell false stories. They tell the truth. I want you to know the truth, and the truth will set you free. What is truth? Jesus said, **"I am the Way, the Truth, and the Life." "He that believes on Me, as the Scriptures have said, out of his innermost being shall flow forth rivers of living water." This He spake of the Spirit that should be given them after Jesus was glorified.** I do not find anything in the Bible but holiness, and nothing in the world but worldliness. Therefore if I live in the world I shall become worldly; but, on the other hand, if I live in the Bible, I shall become holy.

This is the truth, and the truth will set you free. The power of God can we make you. He can actually make you to where you hate sin and love righteousness. He can take away bitterness and hatred and covetousness and malice, and can so consecrate you by His power, through His blood, in nature that you are made pure and every bit holy. Pure in mind, heart and actions. God has given me the way of life, and I want to give it to you, as though this were the last day I had to live. Jesus is the best there is for you, and you can each take Him away with you. God gave His Son to be the propitiation for your sins, and not only so, but also for the sins of the whole world.

Jesus came to make us free from sin and free from disease and pain. When I see any who are diseased and in pain, I have great compassion for them, and when I lay my hands upon them, I know God means men to be so filled with Him that the power of sin shall have no effect upon them, and they shall go forth, as I am doing, to help the needy, sick, and afflicted. But what is the main thing? To preach the Kingdom of God and His righteousness. Jesus came to do this. John came preaching repentance. The disciples began by preaching repentance towards God, and faith in the Lord Jesus Christ, and I tell you, beloved, if you have really been changed by God, there is a repentance in your heart never to be repented of.

Through the revelation of the Word of God we find that divine healing is solely for the glory of God, and salvation is to make you to know that now you have to be inhabited by another, even God, and you have.

## Gifts of Healings and Miracles

***Published in the Pentecostal Evangel, August 4, 1923.***

God has given us much in these last days, and where much is given much will be required. The Lord has said to us, “Ye are the salt of the earth: but if the salt have lost his savor, wherewith shall it be salted? It is thenceforth good for nothing, but to be cast out, and to be trodden under foot of men." We see a thought on the same line when our Lord Jesus says, "If a man abide not in Me, he is cast forth as a branch, and is withered; and men gather them, and cast them into the fire, and they are burned." On the other hand He tells us, "If ye abide in Me, and My words abide in you, ye shall ask what ye will, and it shall be done unto you."

If we do not move on with the Lord these days, and do not walk in the light of revealed truth, we shall become as the savorless salt, as a withered branch. This one thing we must do, forgetting those things that are behind, the past failures and the past blessings, we must reach forth for those things which are before, and press toward the mark for the prize of our high calling of God in Christ Jesus.

For many years the Lord has been moving me on and keeping me from spiritual stagnation. When I was in the Wesleyan Methodist Church I was sure I was saved and was sure I was all right. The Lord said to me, "Come out," and I came out. When I was with the people known as the Brethren I was sure I was all right now. But the Lord said, "Come out." Then I went into the Salvation Army. At that time it was full of life and there were revivals everywhere.

But the Salvation Army went into natural things and the great revivals that they had in those early days ceased. The Lord said to me, "Come out," and I came out. I have had to come out three times since. I believe that this Pentecostal revival that we are now in is the best thing that the Lord has on the earth today, and yet I believe that God has something out of this that is going to be still better. God has no use for any man who is not hungering and thirsting for yet more of Himself and His righteousness.

The Lord has told us to covet earnestly the best gifts, and we need to be covetous for those that will bring Him most glory. We need to see the gifts of healing and the working of miracles in operation today. Some say that it is necessary for us to have the gift of discernment in operation with the gifts of healing, but even apart from this gift I believe the Holy Ghost will have a divine revelation for us as we deal with the sick. Most people seem to have discernment, or think they have, and if they would turn it on themselves for twelve months they would never want to discern again. The gift of discernment is not criticism. I am satisfied that in Pentecostal circles today that our paramount need is more perfect love.

Perfect love will never want the preeminence in everything, it will never want to take the place of another, it will always be willing to take the back seat. If you go to a convention there is always someone who wants to give a message, who wants to be heard. If you have a desire to go to a convention you should have three things settled in your mind. Do I want to be heard? Do I want to be seen? Do I want anything on the line of finances? If I have these things in my heart I have no right to be there. The one thing that must move us must be the constraining love of God to minister for Him. A preacher always loses out when he gets his mind on finances.

It is well for Pentecostal preachers to avoid making much of finances except to stir up people to help our missionaries on financial lines. A preacher who gets big collections for the missionaries need never fear, the Lord will take care of his finances. A preacher should not land at a place and say that God had sent him. I am always fearful when I hear a man advertising this. If he is sent of God, the saints will know it. God has His plans for His servants and we must so live in His plans that He will place us where He wants us.

If you seek nothing but the will of God, He will always put you in the right place at the right time. I want you to see that the gifts of healing and the working of miracles are part of the Spirit's plan and will come forth in operation as we are working along that plan. I must know the movement of the Spirit and the voice of God. I must understand the will of God if I am to see the gifts of the Spirit in operation.

The gifts of healing are so varied. You may go and see ten people and every case is different. I am never happier in the Lord than when I am in a bedroom with a sick person. I have had more revelations of the Lord's presence when I have ministered to the sick at their bedsides than at any other time. It is as your heart goes out to the needy ones in deep compassion that the Lord manifests His presence. You are able to locate their position. It is then that you know that you must be filled with the Spirit to deal with the conditions before you.

Where people are in sickness you find frequently that they are dense about Scripture. They usually know three scriptures though. They know about Paul's thorn in the flesh, and that Paul told Timothy to take a little wine for his stomach's sake, and that Paul left someone sick somewhere; they forget his name, and don't remember the name of the place, and don't know where the chapter is. Most people think they have a thorn in the flesh. The chief thing in dealing with a person who is sick is to locate their exact position. As you are ministering under the Spirit's power the Lord will let you see just that which will be more helpful and most faith-inspiring to them.

When I was in the plumbing business I enjoyed praying for the sick. Urgent calls would come and I would have no time to wash, and with my hands all black I would preach to these sick ones, my heart all aglow with love. Ah, you must have your heart in the thing when you pray for the sick. You have to get right to the bottom of the cancer with a divine compassion and then you will see the gifts of the Spirit in operation.

I was called at 10 o'clock one night to pray for a young person given up by the doctor who was dying of consumption. As I looked, I saw that unless God undertook it was impossible for her to live. I turned to the mother and said, "Well, mother. you will have to go to bed." She said, "Oh, I have not had my clothes off for three weeks." I said to the daughters, "You will have to go to bed," but they did not want to go. It was the same with the son. I put on my overcoat and said, "Good-bye, I'm off." They said, "Oh, don't leave us." I said, "I can do nothing here." They said, "Oh, if you will stop, we will all go to bed." I knew that God would move nothing in an atmosphere of mere natural sympathy and unbelief.

They all went to bed and I stayed, and that was surely a time as I knelt by that bed face to face with death and with the devil. But God can change the hardest situation and make you know that He is almighty.

Then the fight came. It seemed as though the heavens were brass. I prayed from 11 to 3:30 in the morning. I saw the glimmering light on the face of the sufferer and saw her pass away. The devil said, "Now you are done for. You have come from Bradford and the girl has died on your hands." I said, "It can't be. God did not send me here for nothing. This is a time to change strength." I remembered that passage which said, "Men ought always to pray and not to faint." Death had taken place but I knew that my God was all-powerful, and He that had split the Red Sea is just the same today.

It was a time when I would not have "No," and God said "Yes." I looked at the window and at that moment the face of Jesus appeared. It seemed as though a million rays of light were coming from His face. As He looked at the one who had just passed away, the color came back to the face. She rolled over and fell asleep. Then I had a glorious time. In the morning she woke early, put on a dressing gown and walked to the piano. She started to play and to sing a wonderful song. The mother and the sister and the brother had all come down to listen. The Lord had undertaken. A miracle had been wrought.

The Lord is calling us along this way. I am thanking God for difficult cases. The Lord has called us into heart union with Himself; He wants His bride to have one heart and one Spirit with Him and to do what He Himself loved to do. That case had to be a miracle. The lungs were gone, they were just in shreds, but the Lord restored lungs that were perfectly sound.

There is a fruit of the Spirit that must accompany the gift of healing and that is longsuffering. The man who is going through with God to be used in healing must be a man of longsuffering. He must be always ready with a word of comfort. If the sick one is in distress and helpless and does not see everything eye to eye with you, you must bear with him. Our Lord Jesus Christ was filled with compassion and lived and moved in a place of longsuffering, and we will have to get into this place if we are to help needy ones.

There are some times when you pray for the sick and you are apparently rough. But you are not dealing with a person, you are dealing with the Satanic forces that are binding the person. Your heart is full of love and compassion to all, but you are moved to a holy anger as you see the place the devil has taken in the body of the sick one, and you deal with his position with a real forcefulness. One day a pet dog followed a lady out of her house and ran all round her feet. She said to the dog, "My dear, I cannot have you with me today."

The dog wagged its tail and made a big fuss. She said, "Go home, my dear." But the dog did not go. At last she shouted roughly, "Go home," and off it went. Some people deal with the devil like that, The devil can stand all the comfort you like to give him. Cast him out! You are dealing not with the person, you are dealing with the devil. Demon power must be dislodged in the name of the Lord. You are always right when you dare to deal with sickness as with the devil. Much sickness is caused by some misconduct, there is something wrong, there is some neglect somewhere, and Satan has had a chance to get in. It is necessary to repent and confess where you have given place to the devil, and then he can be dealt with.

When you deal with a cancer case, recognize that it is a living evil spirit that is destroying the body. I had to pray for a woman in Los Angeles one time who was suffering with cancer, and as soon as it was cursed it stopped bleeding. It was dead. The next thing that happened was that the natural body pressed it out, because the natural body had no room for dead matter. It came out like a great big ball with tens of thousands of fibers. All these fibers had been pressing into the flesh. These evil powers move to get further hold of the system, but the moment they are destroyed their hold is gone. Jesus said to His disciples that He gave them power to loose and power to bind. It is our privilege in the power of the Holy Ghost to loose the prisoners of Satan and to let the oppressed go free.

Take your position in the first epistle of John and declare, "Greater is He that is in me than he that is in the world." Then recognize that it is not yourself that has to deal with the power of the devil, but the Greater One that is in you. Oh, what it means to be filled with Him. You can do nothing of yourself, but He that is in you will win the victory. Your being has become the temple of the Spirit. Your mouth, your mind, your whole being becomes exercised and worked upon by the Spirit of God.

I was called to a certain town in Norway. The hall seated about 1500 people. When I got to the place it was packed, and hundreds were trying to get in. There were some policemen there. The first thing I did was to preach to the people outside the building. Then I said to the policemen, "It hurts me very much that there are more people outside than inside and I feel I must preach to the people. I would like you to get me the market place to preach in."

They secured for me a great park and a big stand was erected and I was able to preach to thousands. After the preaching we had some wonderful cases of healing. One man came a hundred miles bringing his food with him. He had not been passing anything through his stomach for over a month as he had a great cancer on his stomach. He was healed at that meeting, and opening his parcel, he began eating before all the people.

There was a young woman there with a stiff hand. Instead of the mother making the child use her arm she had allowed the child to keep the arm dormant until it was stiff, and she had grown up to be a young woman and was like the woman that was bowed down with the spirit of infirmity. As she stood before me I cursed the spirit of infirmity in the name of Jesus. It was instantly cast out and the arm was free. Then she waved it all over. At the close of the meeting the devil laid out two people with fits. When the devil is manifesting himself, then is the time to deal with him. Both of these people were delivered, and when they stood up and thanked and praised the Lord what a wonderful time we had.

We need to wake up and be on the stretch to believe God. Before God could bring me to this place He has broken me a thousand times. I have wept, I have groaned, I have travailed many a night until God broke me. It seems to me that until God has mowed you down you never can have this longsuffering for others. We can never have the gifts of healing and the working of miracles in operation only as we stand in the divine power that God gives us and we stand believing God, and having done all we still stand believing.

We have been seeing wonderful miracles these last days and they are only a little of what we are going to see. I believe that we are right on the threshold of wonderful things, but I want to emphasize that all these things will be through the power of the Holy Ghost. You must not think that these gifts will fall upon you like ripe cherries. There is a sense in which you have to pay the price for everything you get. We must be covetous for God's best gifts, and say Amen to any preparation the Lord takes us through, in order that we may be humble, usable vessels through whom He Himself can operate by means of the Spirit's power.

# I am the Lord that Healeth thee

"Is any sick among you? let him call for the elders of the church; and let them pray over him, anointing him with oil in the name of the Lord: and the prayer of faith shall save the sick, and the Lord shall raise him up; and if he have committed sins, they shall be forgiven him" (James 5 :14, 15) .

We have in this precious word a real basis for the truth of healing. In this scripture God gives very definite instructions to the sick. If you are sick, your part is to call for the elders of the church; it is their part to anoint and pray for you in faith, and then the whole situation rests with the Lord. When you have been anointed and prayed for, you can rest assured that the Lord will raise you up. It is the word of God.

I believe that we all can see that the church cannot play with this business. If any turn away from these clear instructions they are in a place of tremendous danger. Those who refuse to obey, do so to their unspeakable loss.

James tells us in connection with this, "if any of you do err from the truth, and one convert him, let him know, that he which converteth the sinner from the error of his ways shall save a soul from death." Many turn away from the Lord, as did King Asa, who sought the physicians in his sickness and consequently died; and I take it that this passage means that if one induces another to turn back to the Lord, he will save such from death and God will forgive a multitude of sins that they have committed. This scripture can also have a large application on the line of salvation. If you turn away from any part of God's truth, the enemy will certainly get an advantage over you.

Does the Lord meet those who look to Him for healing and obey the instructions set forth in James? Most assuredly. Let me tell you a story to show how He will undertake for the most extreme case.

One day I had been visiting the sick, and was with a friend of mine, an architect, when I saw a young man f from his office coming down the road in a car, and holding in his hand a telegram. It contained a very urgent request that we go immediately to pray for a man who was dying. We went off in an auto as fast as possible and in about an hour and a half reached a large house in the country where the man who was dying resided. There were two staircases in that house, and it was extremely convenient, for the doctors could go up and down one, and my friend and I could go up and down the other, and so we had no occasion to meet.

I found on arrival that it was a case of this sort. The man's body had been broken, he was ruptured, and his bowels had been punctured in two places. The discharge from the bowels had formed abscesses, and blood poisoning had set in. The man's face had turned green. Two doctors were in attendance, but they saw that the case was beyond their power. They had telegraphed to London for a great specialist, and, when we arrived, they were at the railway station awaiting his arrival.

The man was very near death and could not speak. I said to his wife, "If you desire, we will anoint and pray for him." She said, "That is why I sent for you." I anointed him in the name of the Lord and asked the Lord to raise him up. Apparently there was no change. (God often hides what He does. From day to day we find that God is doing wonderful things, and we receive reports of healings that have taken place that we heard nothing about at the time of our meetings.

Only last night a woman came into the meeting suffering terribly. Her whole arm was filled with poison, and her blood was so poisoned that it was certain to bring her to her death. We rebuked the thing, and she was here this morning and told us that she was without pain and had slept all night, a thing she had not done for two months. To God be all the praise. You will find He will do this kind of thing all along.)

As soon as we anointed and prayed for this brother we went down the back staircase and the three doctors came up the front staircase. As we arrived downstairs, I said to my friend who had come with me, "Friend let me have hold of your hands." We held each other's hands, and I said to him, "Look into my face and let us agree together, according to Matthew 18:19, that this man shall be brought out of this death." We laid the whole matter before God, and said, "Father, we believe."

Then the conflict began. The wife came down to us and said, "The doctors have got all their instruments out and they are about to operate." I cried, "What? Look here, he's your husband, and I tell you this, if those men operate on him, he will die. Go back and tell them you cannot allow it." She went back to the doctors and said, "Give me ten minutes." They said, "We can't afford to, the man is dying and it is your husband's only chance." She said, "I want ten minutes, and you don't touch his body until I have had them."

They went downstairs by one staircase and we went up by the other. I said to the woman, "This man is your husband, and he cannot speak for himself. It is now the time for you to put your whole trust in God and prove Him wholly true. You can save him from a thousand doctors. You must stand with God and for God in this critical hour." After that, we came down and the doctors went up. The wife faced those three doctors and said, "You shan't touch this man's body. He is my husband. I am sure that if you operate on him he will die, but he will live if you don't touch him."

Suddenly the man in the bed spoke. "God has done it," he said. They rolled back the bed clothes and the doctors examined him, and the abscesses were cut clear away. The nurse cleaned the place where they had been. The doctors could see the bowels still open and they said to the wife, "We know that you have great faith, and we can see that a miracle has taken place.

But you must let us unite these broken parts and put in silver tubes, and we know that your husband will be all right after that, and it need not interfere with your faith at all." She said to them, "God has done the first thing and He can do the rest. No man shall touch him now." And God healed the whole thing. And that man is well and strong today. I can give his name and address to any who want it.

Do you ask by what power this was done? I would answer in the words of Peter, "His name, through faith in His name, made this man strong." The anointing was done in the name of the Lord. And it is written, "The LORD shall raise him up." And He provides the double cure; even if sin has been the cause of the sickness, His Word declares, "If he have committed sins, they shall be forgiven,"

You ask, "What is faith?" Faith is the principle of the Word of God. The Holy Spirit, who inspired the Word, is called the Spirit of Truth, and, as we receive with meekness the engrafted Word, faith springs in our heart-faith in the sacrifice of Calvary: faith in the shed blood of Jesus; faith in the fact that He took our weakness upon Himself, has borne our sicknesses and carried our pains, and that He is our life today.

God has chosen us to help one another. We dare not be independent. He brings us to a place where we submit ourselves to one another. If we refuse to do this, we get away from the Word of

God and out of the place of faith. I have been in this place once and I trust I shall never be there again. I went one time to a meeting. I was very, very sick, and I got worse and worse. I knew the perfect will of God was for me to humble myself and ask the elders to pray for me. I put it off and the meeting finished. I went home without being anointed and prayed with, and everyone in the house caught the thing I was suffering with.

My boys did not know anything else but to trust the Lord as the family Physician, and my youngest boy, George, cried out from the attic, "Dadda, come." I cried, "I cannot come. The whole thing is from me. I shall have to repent and ask the Lord to forgive me." I made up my mind to humble myself before the whole church. Then I rushed to the attic and laid my hands on my boy in the name of Jesus. I placed my hands on his head and the pain left and went lower down; he cried again, "Put your hands still lower."

At last the pain went right down to the feet and as I placed my hand on the feet be was completely delivered. Some evil power had evidently gotten hold and as I laid my hands on the different parts of the body it left. (We have to see the difference between anointing the sick and casting out demons.) God will always be gracious when we humble ourselves before Him and come to a place of brokenness of spirit.

I was at a place one time ministering to a sick woman, and she said, "I'm very sick. I become all right for an hour, and then I have another attack." I saw that it was an evil power that was attacking her, and I learned something in that hour that I had never learned before. As I moved my hand down her body in the name of the Lord that evil power seemed to move just ahead of my hands and as I moved them down further and further the evil power went right out of her body and never returned.

I was in Havre in France and the power of God was being mightily manifested. A Greek named Felix attended the meeting and became very zealous for God. He was very anxious to get all the Catholics he could to the meeting in order that they should see that God was graciously visiting France. He found a certain bed-ridden woman who was fixed in a certain position and could not move, and he told her about the Lord healing at the meetings and that he would get me to come if she wished. She said, “My husband is a Catholic and he would never allow anyone who was not a Catholic to see me.”

She asked her husband to allow me to come and told him what Felix had told her about the power of God working in our midst. He said, “I will have no Protestant enter my house.” She said, “You know the doctors cannot help me, and the priests cannot help, won’t you let this man of God pray for me?” He finally consented and I went to the house. The simplicity of this woman and her child-like faith were beautiful to see.

I showed her my oil bottle and said to her, “Here is oil. It is a symbol of the Holy Ghost. When that comes upon you, the Holy Ghost will begin to work, and the Lord will raise you up.” And God did something the moment the oil fell upon her. I looked toward the window and I saw Jesus. (I have seen Him often. There is no painting that is a bit like Him: no artist can ever depict the beauty of my lovely Lord.) The woman felt the power of God in her body and cried, “I’m free, my hands are free, my shoulders are free, and oh, I see Jesus! I’m free! I’m free!”

The vision vanished and the woman sat up in bed. Her legs were still bound, and I said to her, “I’ll put my hands over your legs and you will be free entirely.” And as I put my hands on those legs covered with bed clothes, I looked and saw the Lord again. She saw Him too and cried, “He’s there again. I’m free! I’m free!” She rose from her bed and walked round the room praising God, and we were all in tears as we saw His wonderful works. The Lord shall raise them up when conditions are met.

When I was a young man I always loved the fellowship of old men, and was always careful to hear what they had to say. I had a friend, an old Baptist minister who was a wonderful preacher. I spent much of my time with him. One day he came to me and said, “My wife is dying.” I said, “Brother Clark, why don’t you believe God? God can raise her up if you will only believe Him.” He asked me to come to his house, and I looked for some one to go with me.

I went to a certain rich man who was very zealous for God, and spent much money in opening up rescue missions, and I asked him to go with me. He said, "Never you mind me. You go yourself, but I don't take to this kind of business." Then I thought of a man who could pray by the hour. When he was on his knees he could go round the world three times and come out at the same place. I asked him to go with me and said to him, "You'll have a real chance this time. Keep at it, and quit when you're through." (Some go on after they are through.)

Brother Nichols, for that was his name, went with me and started praying. He asked the Lord to comfort the husband in his great bereavement and prayed for the orphans and a lot more on this line. I cried, "O my God, stop this man." But there was no stopping him and he went on praying and there was not a particle of faith in anything he uttered. He did stop at last, and I said, "Brother Clark, it's now your turn to pray. He started, "Lord, answer the prayer of my brother and comfort me in this great bereavement and sorrow. Prepare me to face this great trial." I cried out, "My God, stop this man." The whole atmosphere was being charged with unbelief.

I had a glass bottle full of oil and I went up tea the woman and poured the whole lot on her in the name of Jesus. Suddenly Jesus appeared, standing at the foot of the bed. He smiled and vanished. The woman stood up, perfectly healed, and she is a strong woman today.

We have a big God. We have a wonderful Jesus. We have a glorious Comforter. God's canopy is over you and will cover you at all times, preserving you from evil. Under His wings shalt thou trust. The Word of God is living and powerful and in its treasures you will find eternal life. If you dare trust this wonderful Lord, this Lord of life, you will find in Him everything you need.

So many are tampering with drugs, quacks, pills and plasters. Clear them all out and believe God. It is sufficient to believe God. You will find that if you dare trust Him, He will never fail. "The prayer of faith shall save the sick, and the LORD shall raise him up." Do you trust Him? He is worthy to be trusted.

I was one time asked to go to Weston-super-mare, a seaside resort in the West of England. I learned from a telegram that a man had lost his reason and had become a raving maniac, and they wanted me to go to pray for him. I arrived at the place, and the wife said to me, “Will you sleep with my husband?” I agreed, and in the middle of the night an evil power laid hold of him. It was awful. I put my hand on his head and his hair was like a lot of sticks. God gave deliverance-a temporary deliverance. At 6 o’clock the next morning, I felt that it was necessary that I should get out of the house for a short time.

The man saw me going and cried out, “If you leave me, there is no hope.” But I felt that I had to go. As I went out I saw a woman with a Salvation Army bonnet on and I knew that she was going to their 7 o’clock prayer meeting. I said to the Captain who was in charge of the meeting, when I saw he was about to give out a hymn, “Captain, don’t sing. Let’s get to prayer.” He agreed, and I prayed my heart out, and then I grabbed my hat and rushed out of the hall. They all thought they had a madman in their prayer meeting that morning.

I saw the man I had spent the night with, rushing down toward the sea, without a particle of clothing on, about to drown himself. I cried, “In the name of Jesus, come out of him!” The man fell full length on the ground and that evil power went out of him never to return. His wife came rushing after him, and the husband was restored to her in a perfect mental condition.

There are evil powers, but Jesus is greater than all evil powers. There are tremendous diseases, but Jesus is healer. There is no case too hard for Him. The Lion of Judah shall break every chain. He came to relieve the oppressed and to set the captive free. He came to bring redemption, to make us as perfect as man was before the fall.

People want to know how to be kept by the power of God. Every position of grace into which you are led-forgiveness, healing, deliverance of any kind, will be contested by Satan. He will contend for your body. When you are saved, Satan will come round and say, “See, you are not saved.” The devil is a liar. If he says you are not saved, it is a sure sign that you are.

You will remember the story of the man who was swept and garnished. The evil power had been swept out of him. But the man remained in a stationary position. If the Lord heals you, you dare not remain in a stationary position. The evil spirit came back to that man and found the house swept, and took seven others worse than himself, and the last state of that man was worse than the first. Be sure to get filled with God. Get the Occupier. Be filled with the Spirit.

God has a million ways of undertaking for those who go to Him for help. He has deliverance for every captive. He loves you so much that He even says, "Before they call, I will answer." Don't turn Him away.

"I slipped and fell on Broadway, San Diego, in February, 1921, and as was afterwards discovered, fractured the coccyx (the base of the spine), and so severely wrenched the hips and pelvic bones that I became a great sufferer. As the broken bone was not discovered and set until about two months after the accident, the constant pain and irritation caused a general inflammation of the nervous system, and the long delay in getting the bone set, made it impossible to heal, so that, my condition steadily grew worse, and I was taken to the hospital and the bone was removed about a month after it had been set.

Though the wound healed rapidly, the nervous inflammation remained, and so for many months longer I was in constant pain and unable to get around without assistance. I was taken to the first service held by Mr. Wigglesworth on the 2nd of October, 1922. At the close of the service all those who were sick and in pain and had come for healing were requested to rise if possible. My husband assisted me to my feet, and as those were prayed for by the speaker I was instantly healed. How I do not know. I only know the Great Physician touched my body and I was made whole, and freed from pain.

"After I got home I showed how I could sit down and rise with my hands above my head; when before it had taken both hands to push up my feeble body, and I had to have straps on my bed to pull up by. No more use for them now! I lay down and turned over for the first time without pain. I shall never cease to praise God for the healing of my body through the precious blood of Jesus and in His name. I walked to the street car alone the next day and attended the next service and have been "on the go" ever since. Can give names of friends who can substantiate all I have written. To Jesus be all the, praise and glory." - Mrs. Sanders, 4051 Bay View Court, San Diego, Calif.

# CHAPTER NINE

## The grace of longsuffering the counterpart of "gifts of healing."

***The Latter Rain Evangel, April 1923.***
***From "Salvation of God Is All-Inclusive."***

This morning we will move on to the "gifts of healing." "To another, faith by the same Spirit; to another the gifts of healing by the same Spirit." [1Co 12.9]

There is no use expecting to understand the gifts and to understand the epistles unless you have the Holy Ghost. All the epistles are written to a baptized people, and not to the unregenerated. They are written to those who have grown into a maturity as a manifestation of the Christ of God. Do not jump into the epistles before you have come in at the gate of the baptism of the Spirit. I believe that this teaching God is helping me to bring to you will move on you to become restless and discontented on every line till God has finished with you. If we want to know the mind of God through the epistles, there is nothing else to bring the truth but the revelation of the Spirit himself.

He gives the utterance: He opens the door. Don't live in a poverty state when we are all around, in and out, up and down, pressed out beyond measure [2Co 1.8] with the rarest gems of the latest word from God. "Ask, and it shall be given you; seek, and ye shall find; knock, and it shall be opened unto you. For everyone that asketh receiveth; and he that seeketh findeth; and to him that knocketh it shall be opened." [Mt 7.7-8] There is the authority of God's word. And remember, the authority of God's word is Jesus. These are the utterances by the Spirit of Jesus to us this morning.

I come to you with a great inward desire to wake you up to your great possibilities. Your responsibilities will be great, but not as great as your possibilities. You will always find that God is over-abundance on every line he touches for you, and he wants you to come into mind and thought with him so that you are not straightened in yourselves. Be enlarged in God!

[Tongues and interpretation. "It is that which God hath chosen for us, which is mightier than we. It is that which is bottomless, higher than the heights, more lovely than all beside. And God in a measure presses you out to believe all things that you may endure ail things, and lay hold of eternal life through the power of the Spirit."]

The "gifts of healings" are wonderful gifts. There is a difference between having a gift of healing, and "gifts of healings." God wants us not to come behind in anything. I like this word, "gifts of healing." To have the accomplishment of these gifts I must bring myself to a conformity to the mind and will of God in purpose. It would be impossible to have "gifts of healing" unless you possessed that blessed fruit of "longsuffering." You will find these gifts run parallel with that which will bring them into operation without a leak.

But how will it be possible to minister the gifts of healing, considering the peculiarities there are in the Assemblies, and the many evil powers of Satan which confront us and possess bodies? The man who will go through with God and exercise the gifts of healing will have to be a man of longsuffering; always have a word of comfort. If the one who is in distress and helpless doesn't see eye to eye in everything, and doesn't get all he wants, longsuffering will bear and forbear. Longsuffering is a grace Jesus lived in and moved in. He was filled with compassion, and God will never be able to move us to the help of the needy one till we reach that place.

Sometimes you might think by the way I went about praying for the sick that I was unloving and rough; but oh friends, you have no idea what I see behind the sickness and the afflicted. I am not dealing with the person; I am dealing with the satanic forces that are binding the afflicted. As far as the person goes, my heart is full of love and compassion for all, but I fail to see how you will ever reach a place where God will be able definitely to use you until you get angry at the devil.

One day a pet dog followed a lady out of her house and ran all around her feet. She said to the dog, "I cannot have you with me today." The dog wagged its tail and made a great fuss. "Go home, pet," she said, but it didn't go. At last she shouted roughly, "Go home!" and off it went. Some people play with the devil like that. "Poor thing!" The devil can stand ail the comfort anybody in the world could give. Cast him out! You are not dealing with the person; you are dealing with the devil.

If you say, with authority, "Come out, you demons, in the name of the Lord!" they must come out. You will always be right when you dare to treat sickness as the devil's work and you will always be near the mark when you treat it as sin. Let Pentecostal people wake up to see that getting sick is caused by some misconduct; there is some neglect, something wrong somewhere, a weak place where Satan has had a chance to get in. And if we wake up to the real facts of it, we will be ashamed to say that we are sick because people will know we have been sinning.

Gifts of healings are so varied in all lines you will find the gift of discernment often operated in connection therewith. And the manifestations of the Spirit are given to us that we may profit withal. [1Co 12.7] You must never treat a cancer case as anything else than a living, evil spirit which is always destroying the body. It is one of the worst kinds I know. Not that the devil has anything good; every disease of the devil is bad, either to a greater or less degree, but this form of disease is one that you must cast out.

Among the first people I met in Victoria Hall was a woman who had a cancer in the breast. As soon as the cancer was cursed, it stopped bleeding because it was dead. The next thing that happened, the body cast it off, because the natural body has no room for dead matter. When it came out it was like a big ball with thousands of fibers. All these fibers had spread out into the flesh, but the moment the evil power was destroyed they had no power. Jesus gave us power to bind and power to loose; we must bind the evil powers and loose the afflicted and set them free. There are many cases where Satan has control of the mind, and those under satanic influence are not all in asylums.

I will tell you what freedom is: No person in this place who enjoys the fullness of the Spirit with a clear knowledge of redemption, should know that he has a body. You ought to be able to eat and sleep, digest your food, and not be conscious of your body; a living epistle of God's thought and mind, walking up and down the world without pain. That is redemption. To be fully in the will of God, the perfection of redemption, we should not have a pain of any kind.

I have had some experience along this line. When I was weak and helpless and friends were looking for me to die, it was in that straitened place that I saw the fullness of redemption. I read and re-read the 91st Psalm and claimed long life: "With long life will I satisfy him." What else? "And show him my salvation." [Ps 91.16] This is greater than long life. The salvation of God is deliverance from everything, and here I am. At 25 or 30 they were looking for me to die; now at 63 I feel young. So there is something more in this truth that I am preaching than mere words. God hath not designed us for anything else than to be firstfruits, sons of God with power over all the power of the enemy, [Lk 10.19] living in the world but not of it. [Jn 17.16]

We have to be careful in casting out demons, who shall give the command. Man may say "Come out," but unless it is in the Spirit of God our words are vain. The devil always had a good time with me in the middle of the night, and tried to give me a bad time. I had a real conflict with evil powers, and the only deliverance I got was when I bound them in the name of the Lord.

I remember taking a man who was demon-possessed out for a walk one day. We were going through a thickly crowded place and this man became obstreperous. I squared him up and the devil came out of him, but I wasn't careful, and these demons fastened themselves on me right on the street there, so that I couldn't move. Sometimes when I am ministering on the platform and the powers of the devil attack me, the people think I am casting demons out of them, but I am casting them out of myself.

The people couldn't understand when I cast that evil spirit out of that man on the street, but I understood. The man who had that difficulty is now preaching, and is one of the finest men we have. But it required someone to bind the strong man. [Mk 3.27] You must be sure of your ground, and sure it is a mightier power than you that is destroying the devil. Take your position from the first epistle of John and say, "Greater is he that is in me than he that is in the world." [1Jn 4.4] If you think it is you, you make a great mistake. It is your being filled with him; he acting in the place of you; your thought, your mouth, your all becoming exercised by the Spirit of God.

At L----- in Norway we had a place seating 1,500 people. When we reached there it was packed and hundreds were unable to get in. The policemen were standing there, and I thought the first thing I would do would be to preach to the people outside and then go in. I addressed the policemen and said, "You see this condition. I have come with a message to help everybody, and it hurts me very much to find as many people outside as in; I want the promise of you police officials that you will give us the marketplace tomorrow. Will you do it?" They put up their hands that they would.

It was a beautiful day in April, and there was a big stand in the woods about 10 feet high in the great park, where thousands of people gathered. After the preaching we had some wonderful cases of healing. One man came 100 miles, bringing his food with him. He hadn't passed anything through his stomach for over a month for there was a great cancer there. He was healed in the meeting, and opening up his lunch began eating before all the people.

Then there was a young woman who came with a stiff hand. I cursed the spirit of infirmity and it was instantly cast out and the arm was free. She waved it over her head and said, "My father is the chief of police. I have been bound since I was a girl." At the close of the meeting Satan laid out two people with fits. That was my day! I jumped down to where they were and in the name of Jesus delivered them. People said, "Oh isn't he rough," but when they saw those afflicted stand up and praise God, that was a time of rejoicing.

Oh, we must wake up, stretch ourselves out to believe God! Before God could bring me to this place he had to break me a thousand times. I have wept, I have groaned, I have travailed night after night till God broke me. Until God has mowed you down, you will never have this longsuffering for others.

When I was at Cardiff the Lord healed a woman right in the meeting. She was afflicted with ulceration, and while they were singing she fell full length and cried in such a way, I felt something must be done. I knelt down alongside of the woman, laid my hands on her body, and instantly the powers of the devil were destroyed and she was delivered from ulceration; rose up and joined in the singing.

We have been seeing wonderful miracles in these last days, and they are only a little of what we are going to see. When I say "going to see" I do not want to throw something out 10 years to come, nor even two years. I believe we are in the "going," right on the threshold of wonderful things.

You must not think that these gifts fall upon you like ripe cherries. You pay a price for everything you get from God. There is nothing worth having that you do not have to pay for, either temporally or spiritually. I remember when I was at Antwerp and Brussels. The power of God was very mighty upon me there. Coming through to London I called on some friends at C-----. To show you the leading of the Lord, these friends said, "Oh, God sent you here. How much we need you!"

They sent a wire to a place where there was a young man 26 years old, who had been in bed 18 years. His body was so much bigger than an ordinary body, because of inactivity, and his legs were like a child's; instead of bone, there was gristle. He had never been able to dress himself. When they got the wire the father dressed him and he was sitting in a chair. I felt it was one of the opportunities of my life.

I said to this young man, "What is the greatest desire of your heart?" "Oh," he said, "that I might be filled with the Holy Ghost!" I put my hands upon him and said, "Receive, receive ye the Holy Ghost." Instantly he became drunk with the Spirit, and fell off the chair like a big bag of potatoes. I saw what God could do with a helpless cripple. First his head began shaking terrifically; then his back began moving very fast, and then his legs, just like being in a battery.

Then he spoke clearly in tongues, and we wept and praised the Lord. His legs were still as they had been, by all appearances, and this is where I missed it. These "missings" sometimes are God's opportunities of teaching you important lessons. He will teach you through your weaknesses that which is not faith. It was not faith for me to look at that body, but human. The man who will work the works of God must never look at conditions, but at Jesus in whom everything is complete.

I looked at the boy and there was absolutely no help. I turned to the Lord and said, "Lord, tell me what to do," and he did. He said, "Command him to walk, in my name." This is where I missed it. I looked at his conditions and I got the father to help lift him up to see if his legs had strength. We did our best, but he and I together could not move him. Then the Lord showed me my mistake and I said, "God forgive."

I got right down and repented, and said to the Lord, "Please tell me again." God is so good, he never leaves us to ourselves. Again he said to me, "Command him in my name to walk." So I shouted, "Arise and walk in the name of Jesus." Did he do it? No, I declare, he never walked: He was lifted up by the power of God in a moment and he ran. The door was wide open; he ran out across the road into a field where he ran up and down and came back. Oh it was a miracle!

There are miracles to be performed and these miracles will be accomplished by us when we understand the perfect plan of his spiritual graces which has come down to us. These things will come to us when we come to a place of brokenness, of surrender, of wholehearted yieldedness, where we decrease but where God has come to increase; and where we dwell and live in him.

Will you allow him to he the choice of your thoughts? Submit to him, the God of all grace, [1Pe 5.10] that you may be well-furnished with faith for every good work, [2Ti 3.17] that the mind of the Lord may have free course in you, run and be glorified; [2Th 3.1] that the heathen shall know, [Ek 37.28] the uttermost parts of the earth shall be filled with the glory of the Lord as the waters cover the deep. [Ha 2.14]

# YOU DO NOT NEED drugs, quacks, pills and plasters

We have a big God. We have a wonderful Jesus. We have a glorious Comforter. God's canopy is over you and will cover you at all times, preserving you from evil. Under His wings shalt thou trust. The Word of God is living and powerful and in its treasures you will find eternal life. If you dare trust this wonderful Lord, this

Lord of life, you will find in Him everything you need.

So many are tampering with drugs, quacks, pills and plasters. Clear them all out and believe God. It is sufficient to believe God. You will find that if you dare trust Him, He will never fail. "The prayer of faith shall save the sick, and the LORD shall raise him up." Do you trust Him? He is worthy to be trusted.

## Wilt thou be made whole?

Read John 5:1-24

I believe the word of God is so powerful that it can transform any and every life. There is power in God's word to make that which does not appear to appear. There is executive power in the word that proceeds from His lips. The psalmist tells us, "He sent His word and healed them" (Ps. 107:20); and do you think that word has diminished in its power? I tell you nay, but God's word can bring things to pass today as of old.

The psalmist said, "Before I was afflicted I went astray; but now have I kept Thy word." And again, "It is good for me that I have been afflicted; that I might learn Thy statutes" (Ps. 119:67, 71). And if our afflictions will bring us to the place where we see that we cannot live by bread alone, but must partake of every word that proceedeth out of the mouth of God, they will have served a blessed purpose. But I want you to realize that there is a life of purity, a life made clean through the word He has spoken, in which, through faith, you can glorify God with a body that is free from sickness, as well as with a spirit set free from the bondage of Satan.

Here they lay, a great multitude of impotent folk, of blind, halt, withered, around the pool, waiting for the moving of the water. Did Jesus heal everybody? He left many around that pool unhealed. There were doubtless many who had their eyes on the pool and who had no eyes for Jesus. There are many today who have their confidence all the time in things seen. If they would only get their eyes on God instead of on natural things, how quickly they would be helped.

The question arises, 'Is salvation and healing for all?' It is for all who will press right in and get their portion. You remember the case of that Syrophenician woman who wanted the devil cast out of her daughter. Jesus said to her, "Let the children first be filled: for it is not meet to take the children's bread, and to cast it unto the dogs." Note, healing and deliverance are here spoken of by the Master as "the children's bread"; So, if you are a child of God, you can surely press in for your portion.

The Syrophenician woman (Mark 7:24-30) purposed to get from the Lord what she was after, and she said, "Yes, Lord: yet the dogs under the table eat of the children's crumbs." Jesus was stirred as He saw the faith of this woman, and He told her, "For this saying go thy way; the devil is gone out of thy daughter." Today there are many children of God refusing their blood-purchased portion of health in Christ and are throwing it away, while sinners are pressing through and picking it up frown under the table, as it were, and are finding the cure not only for their bodies, but for their spirits and souls as well. The Syrophenician woman went home and found that the devil had indeed gone out of her daughter. Today there is bread, there is life, there is health for every child of God through His all-powerful Word.

The Word can drive every disease away from your body. It is your portion in Christ, Him who is our bread, our life, our health, our all in all. Arid though you may be deep in sin, you can come to Him °n repentance, and He will forgive and cleanse and heal you. His words are spirit and life to those who will receive them. There is a promise in the last verse in Joel, "I will cleanse their blood that I have not cleansed." This is as much as to say He will provide new life within. The life of Jesus Christ, God's Son, can so purify men's hearts and minds that they become entirely transformed, spirit, soul and body.

There they are round the pool; and this man had been there a long time. His infirmity was of thirty-eight years standing. Now and again an opportunity would come, as the angel stirred the waters, but his heart would be made sick as he saw another step in and be healed before him. But one day Jesus was passing that way, and seeing him lying there in that sad condition, enquired, "Wilt thou be made whole?" Jesus said it, and His word is from everlasting to everlasting. This is His word to you, poor, tried and tested one today. You may say, like this poor impotent man, "I have missed every opportunity up till now." Never mind about that-Wilt thou be made whole?

I visited a woman who had been suffering for many years. She was all twisted up with rheumatism and had been two years in bed. I said to her, "What makes you lie here?" She said, "I've come to the conclusion that I have a thorn in the flesh." I said, "To what wonderful degree of righteousness have you attained that you have to have a thorn in the flesh?

Have you had such an abundance of divine revelations that there is danger of your being exalted above measure?" She said, "I believe it is the Lord who is causing me to suffer." I said, "You believe it is the Lord's will for you to suffer, and you are trying to get out of it as quickly as you can. There are doctor's bottles all over the place. Get out of your hiding place and confess that you are a sinner. If you'll get rid of your self-righteousness, God will do something for you. Drop the idea that you are so holy that God has got to afflict you. Sin is the cause of your sickness and not righteousness. Disease is not caused by righteousness, but by sin."

There is healing through the blood of Christ and deliverance for every captive. God never intended His children to live in misery because of some affliction that comes directly from the devil. A perfect atonement was made at Calvary. I believe that Jesus bore my sins, and I am free from them all. I am justified from all things if I dare believe. He Himself took our infirmities and bare our sicknesses; and if I dare believe, I can be healed.

See this poor, helpless man at the pool. "Wilt thou be made whole?" But there is a difficulty in the way. The man has one eye on the pool and one on Jesus. There are many people getting cross-eyed this way these days; they have one eye on the doctor and one on Jesus. If you will only look to Christ and put both your eyes on Him you can be made every whit whole, spirit, soul and body. It is the word of the living God that they that believe should be justified, made free from all things. And whom the Son sets free is free indeed.

You say, "Oh, if I only could believe!" He understands. Jesus knew he had been a long time in that case. He is full of compassion. He knows that kidney trouble, He knows those corns, He knows that neuralgia. There is nothing He does not know. He only wants a chance to show Himself merciful and gracious to you. But He wants to encourage you to believe Him.

If thou canst only believe, thou canst be saved and healed. Dare to believe that Jesus was wounded for your transgressions, was bruised for your iniquities, was chastised that you might have peace, and that by His stripes there is healing for you right here and now. You have failed because you have not believed Him. Cry out to Him even now, "Lord, I believe, help Thou mine unbelief."

I was in Long Beach, California, one day, and with a friend, was passing a hotel. He told me of a doctor there who had a diseased leg; that he had been suffering from it for six years, and could not get out. We went up to his room and found four doctors there. I said, "Well, doctor, I see you have plenty on, I'll call again another day." I was passing at another time, and the Spirit said, "Go join thyself to him." Poor doctor!

He surely was in a bad condition. He said, "I have been like this for six years, and nothing human can help me." I said, "You need God Almighty." People are trying to patch up their lives; but you cannot do anything without God. I talked to him for awhile about the Lord, and then prayed for him. I cried, "Come out of him, in the name of Jesus." The doctor cried, "It's all gone!"

Oh, if we only knew Jesus! One touch of His mightiness meets the need of every crooked thing. The trouble is to get people to believe Him. The simplicity of this salvation is wonderful. One touch of living faith in Him is all that is required, and wholeness is your portion.

I was in Long Beach about six weeks later, and the sick were coming for prayer. Among those filling up the aisle was the doctor. I said, "What is the trouble?" He said, "Diabetes, but it will be all right tonight. I know it will be all right." There is no such thing as the Lord not meeting your need. There are no "if's" or "may's"; His promises are all "shall's." All things are possible to him that believeth. Oh, the name of Jesus! There is power in that name to meet every condition of human need.

At that meeting there was an old man helping his son to the altar. He said, "He has fits-many every day." Then there was a woman with a cancer. Oh, what sin has done! We read that, when God brought forth His people from Egypt, "there was not one feeble person among their tribes" (Ps. 105:37). No disease! All healed by the power of God! I believe that God wants a people like that today.

I prayed for the sister who had the cancer and she said, "I know I'm free and that God has delivered me." Then they brought the boy with the fits, and I commanded the evil spirits to leave, in the name of Jesus. Then I prayed for the doctor. At the next night's meeting the house was full. I called out, "Now, doctor, what about the diabetes?" He said, "It has gone." Then I said to the old man, "What about your son?" He said, "He hasn't had any fits since." We have a God who answers prayer.

Jesus meant this man at the pool to be a testimony forever. When he had both eyes on Jesus, He said to him, "Do the impossible thing. Rise, take up thy bed, and walk." Jesus called on the man with the withered hand to do the impossible-to stretch forth his hand. The man did the impossible thing-he stretched out his hand, and it was made every whit whole.

And so with this impotent man-he began to rise, and he found the power of God moving within. He wrapped up his bed and began to walk off. It was the Sabbath day, and there were some of those folks around who think much more of a day than they do of the Lord; and they began to make a fuss. When the power of God is in manifestation, a protest will always come from some hypocrites. Jesus knew all about what the man was going through, and met him again; and this time He said to him, "Behold, thou art made whole: sin no more, lest a worse thing come unto thee."

There is a close relationship between sin and sickness. How many know that their sickness is a direct result of sin? I hope that no one will come to be prayed for who is living in sin. But if you will obey God and repent of your sin and quit it, God will meet you, and neither your sickness nor your sin will remain. "The prayer of faith shall save the sick, and the Lord shall raise him up; and if he have committed sins, they shall be forgiven him."

Faith is just the open door through which the Lord comes. Do not say, "I was healed by faith." Faith does not save. God saves through that open door. Healing comes the same way. You believe, and the virtue of Christ comes. Healing is for the glory of God. I am here because God healed me when I was dying; and I have been all round the world preaching this full redemption, doing all I can to bring glory to the wonderful name of Jesus, through whom I was healed.

"Sin no more, lest a worse thing come upon thee." The Lord told us in one place about an evil spirit going out from a man. The house that he left got all swept arid garnished, but it received no new occupant. And that evil spirit, with seven other spirits more wicked than himself, went back to that unoccupied house, and the last stage of the man was worse than the first. The Lord does not heal you to go to a baseball game or to a race meet. He heals you for His glory and that from henceforth your life shall glorify Him. But this man remained stationary. He did not magnify God. He did not seek to be filled with the Spirit. And his last state became worse than the first.

The Lord would so cleanse the motive and desires of our hearts that we will seek but one thing only, and that is, His glory. I went to a certain place one day and the Lord said, "This is for My glory." A young man had been sick for along time confined to his bed in an utterly hopeless condition. He was fed only with a spoon, and was never dressed. The weather was damp, and so I said to the people of the house, "I wish you would put the young man's clothes by the fire to air." At first they would not take any notice of my request, but because I was persistent, they at last got out his clothes, and, when they were aired, I took them into his room.

The Lord said to me, "You will have nothing to do with this;" and I just lay out prostrate on the floor. The Lord showed me that He was going to shake the place with His glory. The very bed shook. I laid my hands on the young man in the name of Jesus, and the power fell in such a way that I fell with my face to the floor. In about a quarter of an hour the young man got up and walked up and down praising God.

He dressed himself and then went out to the room where his father and mother were. He said, "God has healed me." Both the father and mother felt prostrate to the floor as the power of God surged through that room. There was a woman in that house who had been in an asylum for lunacy, and her condition was so bad that they were about to take her back. But the power of God healed her, too. The power of God is just the same today as of old. Men need to be taken back to the old paths, to the old-time faith, to believe God's Word and every "Thus saith the Lord" therein. The Spirit of the Lord is moving in these days. God is coming forth. If you want to be in the rising tide, you must accept all God has said.

"Wilt thou be made whole?" It is Jesus who asks it. Give Him your answer. He will hear and He will answer.

# CHAPTER TEN

## What wilt Thou have Me to do?

An Address at The Monday Meeting, Corinthian Hall, Oakland, Cal. Reported by Miss Sadie Cody. October 1914

Published in Triumphs of Faith p. 227-230 October 1914

Read Acts 19. As soon as Paul saw the light from heaven above the brightness of the sun, he said, "Lord, what wilt thou have me to do?" (Acts 9:6). And as soon as he was willing to yield he was in a condition where God could meet his need; where God could display His power; where God could have the man. Oh, beloved, are you saying today, "What wilt thou have me to do?" The place of yieldedness is just where God wants us.

People are saying, "I want the baptism, I want healing, I would like to know of a certainly that I am a child of God," and I see nothing, absolutely nothing in the way except unyieldedness to the plan of God. The condition was met which Paul demanded, and instantly when he laid hands on them they were filled with the Spirit and spake in other tongues and prophesied (Acts 19:6). The only thing needed was just to be in the condition where God could come in. The main thing today that God wants is obedience. When you begin yielding and yielding to God He has a plan for your life, and you come in to that wonderful place where all you have to do is to eat the fruits of Canaan. I am convinced that Paul must have been in divine order as well as those men, and Paul had a mission right away to the whole of Asia.

Brothers and sisters, it is the call of God that counts. Paul was in the call of God. Oh, I believe God wants to stir somebody's heart today to obedience; it may be for China or India or Africa, but the thing God is looking for is obedience.

**"What wilt thou have me to do?"** (Acts 9:6).

...God wrought special miracles by the hands of Paul: so that from his body were brought unto the sick handkerchiefs or aprons, and the diseases departed from them, and the evil spirits went out of them.
Acts 19:11,12

If God can have His way today, the ministry of somebody will begin; it always begins as soon as you yield. Paul had been bringing many people to prison, but God brought Paul to such a place of yieldedness and brokenness that he cried out, "What wilt thou have me to do?" (Acts 9:6). Paul's choice was to be a bondservant for Jesus Christ. Beloved, are you willing that God shall have His way today? God said, "I will shew him how great things he must suffer for my name's sake" (Acts 9:16). But Paul saw that these things were working out a far more exceeding weight of glory. You people who have come for a touch from God, are you willing to follow Him; will you obey Him?

When the prodigal son had returned and the father had killed the fatted calf and made a feast for him, the elder brother was angry and said, "...thou never gavest me a kid, that I might make merry with my friends," (Luke 15:29) but the father said to him, "...all that I have is thine" (v. 31). He could kill a fatted calf at any time. Beloved, all in the Father's house is ours, but it will come only through obedience. And when He can trust us, we will not come behind in anything.

"God wrought special miracles by the hands of Paul" (Acts 19:11). Let us notice the handkerchiefs that went from his body; it means to say that when he touched and sent them forth, God wrought special miracles through them, and diseases departed from the sick, and evil spirits went out of them. Is it not lovely? I believe after we lay hands on these handkerchiefs and pray over them, that they should be handled very sacredly, and even as the one carries them they will bring life, if they are carried in faith to the suffering one. The very effect of it, if you only believed, would change your own body as you carried it.

A woman came to me one day and said, "My husband is such a trial to me; the first salary he gets he spends it in drink, and then he cannot do his work and comes home; I love him very much, what can be done?" I said, "If I were you I would take a handkerchief and would place it under his head when he went to sleep at night, and say nothing to him, but have a living faith." We anointed a handkerchief in the name of Jesus, and she put it under his head.

Oh, beloved, there is a way to reach these wayward ones. The next morning on his way to work he called for a glass of beer; he lifted it to his lips, but he thought there was something wrong with it, and he put it down and went out. He went to another saloon, and another, and did the same thing. He came home sober. His wife was gladly surprised and he told her the story; how it had affected him. That was the turning point in his life; it meant not only giving up drink, but it meant his salvation.

God wants to change our faith today. He wants us to see it is not obtained by struggling and working and pining. "…the Father himself loveth you..." (John 16:27). "...Himself took our infirmities, and bare our sicknesses" (Matthew 8:17). "Come unto me, all ye that labour and are heavy laden, and I will give you rest" (Matthew 11:28).

Who is the man that will take the place of Paul, and yield and yield and yield, until God so possesses him in such a way that from his body virtue shall flow to the sick and suffering? It will have to be the virtue of Christ that flows. Don't think there is some magic virtue in the handkerchief or you will miss the virtue; it is the living faith in the man who lays the handkerchief on his body, and the power of God through that faith. Praise God, we may lay hold of this living faith today. "The blood has never lost its power." As we get in touch with Jesus, wonderful things will take place; and what else? We shall get nearer and nearer to Him.

There is another side to it. "...exorcists, took upon them to call over them which had evil spirits the name of the Lord Jesus, saying, We adjure you by Jesus whom Paul preacheth...and the evil spirit answered and said, Jesus I know, and Paul I know; but who are ye?" (Acts 19:13,15). I beseech you in the name of Jesus, especially those of you who are baptized, to awaken up to the fact that you have power if God is with you; but there must be a resemblance between you and Jesus. The evil spirit said, "…Jesus I know, and Paul I know; but who are ye?" (Acts 19:15). Paul had the resemblance.

You are not going to get it without having His presence; His presence changes you. You are not going to be able to get the results without the marks of the Lord Jesus. The man must have the divine power within himself; devils will take no notice of any power if they do not see the Christ. "Jesus I know, and Paul I know; but who are ye?" The difference between these men was they had not the marks of Christ, so the manifestation of the power of Christ was not seen.

You want power: don't take the wrong way. Don't take it as power because you speak in tongues, and if God has given you revelations along certain lines don't take that for the power; or if you have even laid hands on the sick and they have been healed, don't take that for the power. "The Spirit of the Lord is upon me..."

(Luke 4:18); that alone is the power. Don't be deceived; there is a place to get where you know the Spirit is upon you, so you will be able to do the works which are wrought by this blessed Spirit of God in you, and the manifestation of His power shall be seen, and people will believe in the Lord.

What will make men believe the divine promises of God? Beloved, let me say to you today, God wants you to be ministering spirits, and it means to be clothed with another power. And this divine power, you know when it is there, and you know when it goes forth. The baptism of Jesus must bring us to have a single eye to the glory of God; everything else is wasted time and wasted energy. Beloved, we can reach it; it is a high mark but we can get to it. You ask how? "What wilt thou have me to do?" That is the plan. It means a perfect surrender to the call of God, and perfect obedience.

A dear young Russian came to England. He did not know the language, but learned it quickly and was very much used and blessed of God; and as the wonderful manifestations of the power of God were seen, they pressed upon him to know the secret of his power, but he felt it was so sacred between him and God he should not tell it, but they pressed him so much he finally said to them: "First God called me, and His presence was so precious, that I said to God at every call I would obey Him, and I yielded, and yielded, and yielded, until I realized that I was simply clothed with another power altogether, and I realized that God took me, tongue, thoughts and everything, and I was not myself but it was Christ working through me."

How many of you today have known that God has called you over and over, and has put His hand upon you, but you have not yielded? How many of you have had the breathing of His power within you, calling you to prayer, and you have to confess you have failed?

I went to a house one afternoon where I had been called, and met a man at the door. He said, "My wife has not been out of bed for eight months; she is paralyzed. She has been looking so much for you to come, she is hoping God will raise her up." I went in and rebuked the devil's power. She said, "I know I am healed; if you go out I will get up." I left the house, and went away not hearing anything more about her. I went to a meeting that night, and a man jumped up and said he had something he wanted to say; he had to go to catch a train but wanted to talk first. He said, "I come to this city once a week, and I visit the sick all over the city. There is a woman I have been visiting and I was very much distressed about her; she was paralyzed and has lain on that bed many months, and when I went there today she was up doing her work." I tell this story because I want you to see Jesus.

We had a letter which came to our house to say that a young man was very ill. He had been to our Mission a few years before with a very bad foot; he had no shoe on, but a piece of leather fastened on the foot. God healed him that day. Three years after, something else came upon him. What it was I don't know, but his heart failed, and he was helpless; he could not rise or dress or do anything for himself, and in that condition he called his sister and told her to write and see if I would pray.

My wife said to go, and she believed God would give me that life. I went, and when I got to this place I found the whole country was expecting me; they had said that when I came this man would be healed. I said to the woman when I arrived, "I have come." "Yes," she said, "but it is too late." "Is he alive?" I asked, "Yes, just alive," she said. I went in and put my hands upon him, and said, "Martin." He just breathed slightly, and whispered, "The doctor said if I move from this position I will never move again." I said, "Do you know the Scripture says, 'God is the strength of my heart, and my portion for ever'?" (Psalm 73:26). He said, "Shall I get up?" I said, "No."

That day was spent in prayer and ministering the Word. I found a great state of unbelief in that house, but I saw Martin had faith to be healed. His sister was home from the asylum. God held me there to pray for that place. I said to the family, "Get Martin's clothes ready; I believe he is to be raised up." I felt the unbelief. I went to the chapel and had prayer with a number of people around there, and before noon they too believed Martin would be healed. When I returned I said, "Are his clothes ready?" They said, "No." I said, "Oh, will you hinder God's work in this house?" I went in to Martin's room all alone. I said, "I believe God will do a new thing today. I believe when I lay hands on you the glory of heaven will fill the place."

I laid my hands on him in the name of the Father, Son, and Holy Ghost, and immediately the glory of the Lord filled the room, and I went headlong to the floor. I did not see what took place on the bed, or in the room, but this young man began to shout out, "Glory, glory!" and I heard him say, "for Thy glory, Lord," and that man stood before me perfectly healed. He went to the door and opened it and his father stood there. He said, "Father, the Lord has raised me up," and the father fell to the floor and cried for salvation. The young woman brought out of the asylum was perfectly healed at that moment by the power of God in that house.

God wants us to see that the power of God coming upon people has something more in it than we have yet known. The power to heal and to baptize is in this place, but you must say, "Lord, what wilt thou have me to do?" You say it is four months before the harvest. If you had the eyes of Jesus you would see that the harvest is already here. The devil will say you can't have faith; you tell him he is a liar. The Holy Ghost wants you for the purpose of manifesting Jesus through you. Oh, may you never be the same again! The Holy Spirit moving upon us will make us to be like Him, and we will truly say, "Lord, what wilt thou have me to do?" Whom the Lord loveth.

## **Way to Overcome: Believe!** 1917

First John 5. The greatest weakness in the world is unbelief. The greatest power is the faith that works by love. Love, mercy, and grace are bound eternally to faith. There is no fear in love and no question as to being caught up when Jesus comes. The world is filled with fear, torment, remorse, and brokenness, but faith and love are sure to overcome. "Who is he that overcomes the world, but he that believes that Jesus is the Son of God?" (1 John 5:5). God hath established the earth and humanity on the lines of faith. As you come into line, fear is cast out, the Word of God comes into operation and you find bedrock. The way to overcome is to believe Jesus is the Son of God. The commandments are wrapped up in it.

When there is a fidelity between you and God and the love of God is so real that you feel you could do anything for Jesus, all the promises are yea and amen to those who believe. Your life is centered there. Always overcoming what is in the world.

Who keeps the commandments? The born of God. "Ye are of God, little children, and have overcome them: because greater is he that is in you, than he that is in the world" (1 John 4:4). They that believe, love. When did He love us? When we were in the mire. What did He say? Thy sins are forgiven thee. Why did He say it? Because He loved us. What for? That He might bring many sons into glory. His object? That we might be with Him forever. All the pathway is an education for this high vocation and calling.

This hidden mystery of love to us, the undeserving! For our sins the double blessing. "...whatsoever is born of God overcomes the world: and this is the victory...even our faith" (1 John 5:4). He who believes – to believe is to overcome. On the way to Emmaus Jesus, beginning from Moses and all the prophets, interpreted to them in all the Scriptures the things concerning Himself (Luke 24:27). He is the root! In Him is life. When we receive Christ, we receive God and the promises (Galatians 3:29), that we might receive the promise of the Spirit through faith. I am heir to all the promises because I believe. A great heirship! I overcome because I believe the truth. The truth makes me free.

TONGUES AND INTERPRETATION: "It is God who exalts, God who makes rich. The Lord in His mighty arms bears thee up – it is the Lord that encompasses round about thee. When I am weak, then I am strong."

No wavering! This is the principle. He who believes is definite, and because Jesus is in it, it will come to pass. He is the same yesterday, today, and forever (Hebrews 13:8). They that are poor in spirit are heirs to all. There is no limit to the power, for God is rich to all who call upon Him. Not the will of the flesh, but of God (John 1:13). Put in your claim for your children, your families, your co-workers, that many sons may be brought to glory (Hebrews 2:10), for it is all on the principle of faith. There is nothing in my life or ambition equal to my salvation, a spiritual revelation from heaven according to the power of God, and it does not matter how many flashlights Satan sends through the human mind; roll all on the blood.

Who overcomes? He who believes Jesus is the Son (1 John 5:5). God calls in the person with no credentials, it's the order of faith, He who believes overcomes – will be caught up. The Holy Ghost gives revelation all along the line. He that is not against us is for us, and some of the most godly have not touched Pentecost yet. We must have a good heart especially to the household of faith. "...If any man love the world, the love of the Father is not in him" (1 John 2:15). The root principle of all truth in the human heart is Christ, and when grafted deeply there are a thousand lives you may win. Jesus is the way, the truth, and the life (John 14:6), the secret to every hard problem in the world.

You can't do it! Joseph could not! Everything depends on the principles in your heart. If God dwells in us the principle is light, it comprehends darkness. If thine eye be single, thy whole body shall be full of light, breaking through the hardest thing. "Herein is our love made perfect, that we may have boldness in the day of judgment: because as he is, so are we in this world (1 John 4:17) – for faith has full capacity. When man is pure and it is easy to detect darkness, he that hath this hope purifies himself (1 John 3:3).

TONGUES AND INTERPRETATION: "God confirms in us faith that we may be refined in the world, having neither spot nor blemish nor any such thing. It is all on the line of faith, he that hath faith overcomes – it is the Lord Who purifies and bringeth where the fire burns up all the dross, and anoints with fresh oil; see to it that ye keep pure. God is separating us for Himself.

"…I will give you a mouth and wisdom, which all your adversaries will not be able to gainsay nor resist" (Luke 21:15). The Holy Spirit will tell you in the moment what you shall say. The world will not understand you, and you will find as you go on with God that you do not under-stand fully. We cannot comprehend what we are saved to, or from. None can express the joy of God's indwelling. The Holy Spirit can say through you the need of the moment. The world knows us not because it knew Him not.

"Who is he that overcomes the world, but he that believes Jesus is the Son of God?" (1 John 5:5). A place of confidence in God, a place of prayer, a place of knowledge, that we have what we ask, because we keep His commandments and do the things that are pleasing in His sight. Enoch before his translation had the testimony, he had been well-pleasing unto God. We overcome by believing.

First Published in Flames of Fire p. 2 March 1917

# Way of faith

***Published in the Pentecostal Evangel, June 15, 1935.***

In Romans 4:16 we read, "It is of faith, that it might be by grace," meaning that we can open the door and God will come in. What will happen if we really open the door by faith? God is greater than our thoughts. He puts it to us, "Exceeding abundantly above all that we ask or think." When we ask a lot, God says "more." Are we ready for the "more"? And then the "much more"? We may be, or we may miss it. We may be so endued by the Spirit of the Lord in the morning that it shall be a tonic for the whole day. God can so thrill us with new life that nothing ordinary or small will satisfy us after that. There is a great place for us in God where we won't be satisfied with small things. We won't have any satisfaction unless the fire falls, and whenever we pray we will have the assurance that what we have prayed for is going to follow the moment we open our mouth. Oh this praying in the Spirit! This great plan of God for us! In a moment we can go right in. In where? Into His will. Then all things will be well.

You can't get anything asleep these days. The world is always awake, and we should always be awake to what God has for us. Awake to take! Awake to hold it after we get it! How much can you take? We know that God is more willing to give than we are to receive. How shall we dare to be asleep when the Spirit commands us to take everything on the table. It is the greatest banquet that ever was and ever will be—the table where all you take only leaves more behind. A fullness that cannot be exhausted! How many are prepared for a lot?

"And Jesus entered into Jerusalem, and into the temple: and when he had looked round about upon all things, and now the eventide was come, he went out unto Bethany with the twelve. And on the morrow, when they were come from Bethany, he was hungry: and seeing a fig tree afar off having leaves, he came, if haply he might find any thing thereon: and when he came to it, he found nothing but leaves; for the time of figs was not yet. And Jesus answered and said, No man eat fruit of thee hereafter for ever. And his disciples heard it." Mark 11:11-14.

Jesus was sent from God to meet the world's need. Jesus lived to minister life by the words He spoke. He said to Philip, "He that hath seen me hath seen the Father… the words that I speak unto you, I speak not of myself: but the Father that dwelleth in me." I am persuaded that if we are filled with His words of life and the Holy Ghost, and Christ is made manifest in our mortal flesh, then the Holy Ghost can really move us with His life, His words, till as He was, so are we in the world. We are receiving our life from God, and it is always kept in tremendous activity, working in our whole nature as we live in perfect contact with God.

Jesus spoke, and everything He said must come to pass. That is the great plan. When we are filled only with the Holy Spirit, and we won't allow the Word of God to be detracted by what we hear or by what we read, then comes the inspiration, then the life, then the activity, then the glory! Oh to live in it! To live in it is to be moved by it. To live in it is to be moved so that we will have God's life, God's personality in the human body.

By the grace of God I want to impart the Word, and bring you into a place where you will dare to act upon the plan of the Word, to so breathe life by the power of the Word that it is impossible for you to go on under any circumstances without His provision. The most difficult things that come to us are to our advantage from God's side. When we come to the place of impossibilities it is the grandest place for us to see the possibilities of God. Put this right in your mind and never forget it. You will never be of any importance to God till you venture in the impossible. God wants people on the daring line. I do not mean foolish daring. "Be filled with the Spirit," and when we are filled with the Spirit we are not so much concerned about the secondary thing. It is the first with God.

Everything of evil, everything unclean, everything Satanic in any way is an objectionable thing to God, and we are to live above it, destroy it, not to allow it to have any place. Jesus didn't let the devil answer back. We must reach the place where we will not allow anything to interfere with the plan of God.

Jesus and His disciples came to the tree. It looked beautiful. It had the appearance of fruit, but when He came to it He found nothing but leaves. He was very disappointed. Looking at the tree, He spoke to it: Here is shown forth His destructive power, "No man eat fruit of thee hereafter for ever." The next day they were passing by the same way and the disciples saw the tree "dried up from the roots." They said to Jesus, "Behold, the fig tree which thou cursedst is withered away." And Jesus said, "Have faith in God."

There isn't a person that has ever seen a tree dried from the root. Trees always show the first signs of death right at the top. But the Master had spoken. The Master dealt with a natural thing to reveal to these disciples a supernatural plan. If He spoke it would have to obey. And, God, the Holy Ghost, wants us to understand clearly that we are the mouthpiece of God and are here for His divine plan. We may allow the natural mind to dethrone that, but in the measure we do, we won't come into the treasure which God has for us. The Word of God must have first place. It must not have a second place. In any measure that we doubt the Word of God, from that moment we have ceased to thrive spiritually and actively. The Word of God is not only to be looked at and read, but received as the Word of God to become life right within our life. "Thy word have I hid in my heart that I might not sin against thee."

"I give unto you power… over all the power of the enemy." Luke 10:19. There it is. We can accept or reject it. I accept and believe it. It is a word beyond all human calculation: "Have faith in God." These disciples were in the Master's schooL They were the men who were to turn the world upside down. As we receive the Word we will never be the same; if we dare to act as the Word goes forth and not be afraid, then God will honor us. "The Lord of hosts is with us; the God of Jacob is our refuge." Jacob was the weakest of all, in any way you like to take it. He is the God of Jacob, and He is our God. So we may likewise have our names changed to Israel.

As the Lord Jesus injected this wonderful word, "Have faith in God," into the disciples, He began to show how it was to be. Looking around about Him He saw the mountains, and He began to bring a practical application. A truth means nothing unless it moves us. We can have our minds filled a thousand times, but it must get into our hearts if there are to be any results. All inspiration is in the heart. All compassion is in the heart.

Looking at the mountains He said, "Shall not doubt in his heart." That is the barometer. You know exactly where you are. The man knows when he prays. If his heart is right how it leaps. No man is any good for God and never makes progress in God who does not hate sin. You are never safe. But there is a place in God where you can love righteousness and where you can hate iniquity till the Word of God is a light in your bosom, quickening every fiber of your body, thrilling your whole nature. The pure in heart see God. Believe in the heart! What a word! If I believe in my heart God says I can begin to speak, and "whatsoever" I say shall come to pass.

Here is an act of believing in the heart. I was called to Halifax, England, to pray for a lady missionary. I found it an urgent call. I could see there was an absence of faith, and I could see there was death: Death is a terrible thing, and God wants to keep us alive. I know it is appointed unto man once to die, but I believe in a rapturous death. I said to the woman, "How are you?" She said, "I have faith," in a very weak tone of voice. "Faith? Why you are dying? Brother Walshaw, is she dying?" "Yes." "Nurse, is she dying?" "Yes." To a friend standing by, "Is she dying?" "Yes."

Now I believe there is something in a heart that is against defeat, and this is the faith which God hath given to us. I said to her, "In the name of Jesus, now believe and you'll live." She said, "I believe," and God sent life from her head to her feet. They dressed her and she lived.

"Have faith." It isn't saying you have faith. It is he that believeth in his heart. It is a grasping of the eternal God. Faith is God in the human vessel. "This is the victory that overcometh the world, even our faith." 1 John 5:4. He that believeth overcomes the world. "Faith cometh by hearing, and hearing by the Word of God." He that believeth in his heart! Can you imagine anything easier than that? He that believeth in his heart! What is the process? Death! No one can live who believes in his heart. He dies to everything worldly. He that loves the world is not of God. You can measure the whole thing up, and examine yourself to see if you have faith. Faith is a life. Faith enables you to lay hold of that which is and get it out of the way for God to bring in something that is not.

Just before I left home I was in Norway. A woman wrote to me from England saying she had been operated on for cancer three years before, but that it was now coming back. She was living in constant dread of the whole thing as the operation was so painful.

Would it be possible to see me when I returned to England? I wrote that I would be passing through London on the 20th of June last year. If she would like to meet me at the hotel I would pray for her. She replied that she would be going to London to be there to meet me. When I met this woman I saw she was in great pain, and I have great sympathy for people who have tried to get relief and have failed. If you preachers lose your compassion you can stop preaching, fof it won't be any good.

You will only be successful as a preacher as you let your heart become filled with the compassion of Jesus. As soon as I saw her I entered into the state of her mind. I saw how distressed she was. She came to me in a mournful spirit, and her whole face was downcast. I said to her, "There are two things going to happen today. One is that you are to know that you are sayed." "Oh, if I could only know I was saved," she said. "There is another thing. You have to go out of this hotel without a pain, without a trace of the cancer."

Then I began with the Word. Oh this wonderful Word! We do not have to go up to bring Him down; neither do we have to go down to bring Him up. "The word is nigh thee, even in thy mouth, and in thy heart: that is, the word of faith, which we preach." Romans 10:8. I said, "Believe that He took your sins when He died at the cross. Believe that when He was buried, it was for you. Believe that when He arose, it was for you. And now at God's right hand He is sitting for you. If you can believe in your heart and confess with your mouth, you shall be saved." She looked at me saying, "Oh, it is going all through my body. I know I am saved now. If He comes today, I'll go. How I have dreaded, the thought of His coming all my life! But if He comes today, I know I shall be ready."

The first thing was finished. Now for the second. I laid my hands upon her in the name of Jesus, believing in my heart that I could say what I wanted and it should be done. I said, "In the name of Jesus, I cast this out." She jumped up. "Two things have happened," she said. "I am saved and now the cancer is gone."

**Faith will stand amid the wrecks of time,**

**Faith unto eternal glories climb;**

**Only count the promise true,**

**And the Lord will stand by you—**

**Faith will win the victory every time!**

So many people have nervous trouble. I'll tell you how to get rid of your nervous trouble. I have something in my bag, one dose of which will cure you. "I am the Lord that healeth thee." How this wonderful Word of God changes the situation. "Perfect love casteth out fear." "There is no fear in love." I have tested that so often, casting out the whole condition of fear and the whole situation has been changed. We have a big God, only He has to be absolutely and only trusted. The people who really do believe God are strong, and "he that hath clean hands shall be stronger and stronger."

At the close of a certain meeting a man said to me, "You have helped everybody but me. I wish you would help me." "What's the trouble with you?" "I cannot sleep because of nervous trouble. My wife says she has not known me to have a full night's sleep for three years. I am just shattered." Anybody could tell he was. I put my hands upon him and said, **"Brother I believe in my heart. Go home and sleep in the name of Jesus."** "I can't sleep." **"Go home and sleep in the name of Jesus."** "I can't sleep."

The lights were being put out, and I took the man by the coat collar and said, "Don't talk to me anymore." That was sufficient. He went after that, When he got home his mother and wife said to him, "What has happened?" "Nothing. He helped everybody but me." "Surely he said something to you." "He told me to come home and sleep in the name of Jesus, but you know I can't sleep in anything."

His wife urged him to do what I had said, and he had scarcely got his head on the pillow before the Lord put him to sleep. The next morning he was still asleep. The next morning he was still asleep. She began to make a noise in the bedroom to awaken him, but he did not waken. Sunday morning he was still asleep. She did what every good wife would do. She decided to make a good Sunday dinner, and then awaken him. After the dinner was prepared she went up to him and put her hand on his shoulder and shook him, saying, "Are you never going to wake up?" From that night that man never had any more nervousness.

A man came to me for whom I prayed. Then I asked, "Are you sure you are perfectly healed?" "Well," he said, "there is just a little pain in my shoulder." "Do you know what that is?" I asked him. "That is unbelief. Were you saved before you believed or after?" "After." "You will be healed after." "It is all right now," he said, It was all right before, but he hadn't believed.

The Word of God is for us. It is by faith that it might be by grace.

## To Be Like Jesus

The word of God is living and powerful, and sharper than any two-edged sword, piercing even to the division of soul and spirit...and is a discerner of the thoughts and intents of the heart.

--Hebrews 4:12

Scripture reading: Philippians 2:1-22

We have yet to see the forcefulness of the Word of God. The Word, the life, the presence, the power is in your body, in the very marrow of your bones, and absolutely everything else must be discharged. Sometimes we do not fully reflect on this wonderful truth: the Word, the life, the Christ who is the Word divides you from soul affection, from human weakness, from all depravity. The blood of Jesus can cleanse you until your soul is purified and your nature is destroyed by the nature of the living Christ.

In Christ, we have encountered divine resurrection touches. In the greatest work God ever did on the face of the earth, Christ was raised from the dead by the operation of the power of God. As the resurrection of Christ operates in our hearts, it will dethrone wrong things and will build right things. Callousness will have to change; hardness will have to disappear; all evil thoughts will have to go. In the place of these will be lowliness of mind.

What beautiful cooperation with God in thought and power and holiness! The Master "made Himself of no reputation" (Phil. 2:7). He absolutely left the glory of heaven, with all its wonder. He left it and submitted Himself to humiliation. He went down, down, down into death for one purpose only: that He might destroy the power of death, even the Devil, and deliver those people who all their lifetime have been subject to fear--deliver them from the fear of death and the Devil (Heb. 2:14-15).

How will this wonderful plan come to pass? By transformation, resurrection, thoughts of holiness, intense zeal, desire for all of God, until we live and move in the atmosphere of holiness.

**Thought for today: If you will let go, God will take hold and keep you up.**

## How to Live in the Miraculous!

This is a quick explanation of how to live and move in the realm of the miraculous. Seeing divine interventions of God is not something that just spontaneously happens because you have been born-again. There are certain biblical principles and truths that must be evident in your life. This is a very basic list of some of these truths and laws:

1. You must give Jesus Christ your whole heart. You cannot be lackadaisical in this endeavour. Being lukewarm in your walk with God is repulsive to the Lord. He wants 100% commitment. Jesus gave His all, now it is our turn to give our all. He loved us 100%. Now we must love Him 100%.

***My son, give me thine heart, and let thine eyes observe my ways (Proverbs 23:26).***

***So then because thou art lukewarm, and neither cold nor hot, I will spew thee out of my mouth (Revelation 3:16).***

2. There must be a complete agreement with God's Word. We must be in harmony with the Lord in our attitude, actions, thoughts, and deeds. Whatever the Word of God declares in the New Testament is what we wholeheartedly agree with.

***Can two walk together, except they be agreed? (Amos 3:3).***

***For the eyes of the LORD run to and fro throughout the whole earth, to shew himself strong in the behalf of them whose heart is perfect toward him (2 Chronicles 16:9).***

3. Obey and do the Word from the heart, from the simplest to the most complicated request or command. No matter what the Word says to do, do it! Here are some simple examples: Lift your hands in praise, in everything give thanks, forgive instantly, gather together with the saints, and give offerings to the Lord, and so on.

***I can of mine own self do nothing: as I hear, I judge: and my judgment is just; because I seek not mine own will, but the will of the Father which hath sent me (John 5:30).***

4. Make Jesus the highest priority of your life. Everything you do, do not do it as unto men, but do it as unto God.

***If ye then be risen with Christ, seek those things which are above, where Christ sitteth on the right hand of God.***

***Set your affection on things above, not on things on the earth (Colossians 3:1-2).***

5. Die to self! The old man says, "My will be done!" The new man says, "God's will be done!"

   ***I am crucified with Christ: nevertheless I live; yet not I, but Christ liveth in me: and the life which I now live in the flesh I live by the faith of the Son of God, who loved me, and gave himself for me (Galatians 2:20).***

   ***Now if we be dead with Christ, we believe that we shall also live with him (Romans 6:8).***

6. Repent the minute you get out of God's will—no matter how minor, or small the sin may seem.

   ***(Revelation 3:19).***

   ***As many as I love, I rebuke and chasten: be zealous therefore, and repent.***

7. Take one step at a time. God will test you (not to do evil) to see if you will obey him. *Whatever He tells you to do: by His Word, by His Spirit, or within your conscience, do it.* He will never tell you to do something contrary to His nature or His Word!

   ***For whosoever shall do the will of my Father which is in heaven, the same is my brother, and sister, and mother (Matthew 12:50).***

   ***Then went he down, and dipped himself seven times in Jordan, according to the saying of the man of God: and his flesh came again like unto the flesh of a little child, and he was clean (2 Kings 5:14).***

## ABOUT THE AUTHOR

**Michael met and married his wonderful wife (Kathleen) in 1978. As a direct result of the Author and his wife's personal, amazing experiences with God, they have had the privilege to serve as pastors/apostles, missionaries, evangelist, broadcasters, and authors for over four decades. By Gods Divine enablement's and Grace, Doc Yeager has written over 70 books, ministered over 10,000 Sermons, and having helped to start over 25 churches. His books are filled with hundreds of their amazing testimonies of Gods protection, provision, healing's, miracles, and answered prayers. They flow in the gifts of the Holy Spirit, teaching the word of God, wonderful signs following and confirming God's word. Websites Connected to Doc Yeager.**

www.docyeager.com

www.jilmi.org

www.wbntv.org

**Some of the Books Written by Doc Yeager:**

**"Living in the Realm of the Miraculous – "1 to 5 "**
**"I need God Cause I'm Stupid"**
**"The Miracles of Smith Wigglesworth"**
**"How Faith Comes 28 WAYS"**
**"Horrors of Hell, Splendors of Heaven"**
**"The Coming Great Awakening"**
**"Sinners in The Hands of an Angry GOD",**
**"Brain Parasite Epidemic"**
**"My JOURNEY to HELL" - illustrated for teenagers**
**"Divine Revelation of Jesus Christ"**
**"My Daily Meditations"**
**"Holy Bible of JESUS CHRIST"**
**"War In The Heavenlies - (Chronicles of Micah)"**
**"My Legal Rights to Witness"**
**"Why We (MUST) Gather! - 30 Biblical Reasons"**
**"My Incredible, Supernatural, Divine Experiences"**
**"How GOD Leads & Guides! - 20 Ways"**
**"Weapons of Our Warfare"**
**"How You Can Be Healed"**
**"Hell Is For Real"**
**"Heaven Is For Real"**
**"God Still Heals"**
**"God Still Provides"**
**"God Still Protects"**
**"God Still Gives Dreams & Visions"**
**"God Still Does Miracles"**
**"God Still Gives Prophetic Words"**
**"Life Changing Quotes of Smith Wigglesworth"**

Made in United States
Orlando, FL
27 March 2025

59893564R00095